THE FICTION OF BHARATI MUKHERJEE

A Cultural Perspective

Nagendra Kumar

ATLANTIC
PUBLISHERS & DISTRIBUTORS (P) LTD

Published by

ATLANTIC

PUBLISHERS & DISTRIBUTORS (P) LTD

7/22, Ansari Road, Darya Ganj,
New Delhi-110002
Phones : +91-11-40775252, 23273880, 23275880, 23280451
Fax : +91-11-23285873
Web : www.atlanticbooks.com
E-mail : orders@atlanticbooks.com

Branch Office
5, Nallathambi Street, Wallajah Road,
Chennai-600002
Phones : +91-44-64611085, 32413319
E-mail : chennai@atlanticbooks.com

Printed in India at Nice Printing Press, A-33/3A, Site-IV, Industrial Area, Sahibabad, Ghaziabad, U.P.

PREFACE

Bharati Mukherjee is one of the major novelists of Indian diaspora who have achieved enviable positions within a comparatively short creative span. The creative odyssey that started with the publication of *The Tiger's Daughter* (1972) kept her seriously involved in exploring the complexities of his choicest theme of expatriate experience. Since then she has never looked back and her literary accomplishments have manifested themselves in the five novels and two story collections that have appeared so far. It is a matter of concern that writer of her potentiality and acumen has not received the critical attention she deserves in that no full-length volume has been published on her as yet. A review of the existing critical scholarship demonstrates that she has been devoted a chapter or two in critical works on expatriate writers. Such research articles do touch upon the significant components of her creative personality but they fail to provide a totality of vision in view of their narrow scope. Emmanuel S. Nelson's *Bharati Mukherjee : Critical Perspectives* (1993) is a collection of perceptive essays which, however, excludes Mukherjee's two major latest works — *The Holder of the World* and *Leave It to Me*. The present volume aims at filling in this serious gap in critical literature on Bharati Mukherjee by taking into consideration her entire creative output.

Worked out in six chapters, the volume opens with Introduction which takes up the major concepts of culture as propounded by T.S. Eliot, Raymond Williams and Terry Eagleton among others. It also defines certain key terms like acculturation, assimilation, satellite culture, etc., which have been invariably employed by the artists to express the quality of expatriate experience. The second chapter titled "The Shaping of Creative Sensibility" is an exhaustive account of Mukherjee's development as a creative artist. With a view to ensure a proper appreciation of her talents, the distinctive features of her personal life have been enumerated and her academic achievements frequently underlined. The major formative influences like V.S. Naipaul and Bernard Malamud among others have been discussed and the nature of their impact commented upon. It has been argued that Mukherjee outgrew her models one after the other and matured into a writer of acknowledged credentials by her innate artistic proclivities.

Mukherjee's fictional writings have been analysed in three well-marked phases — The Phase of Expatriation, The phase of Transition and The Phase of Immigration. The first phase of her development from 1972 to 1979 conveniently termed Expatriation forms the content of the third chapter. During this period her two early novels, *The Tiger's Daughter* (1972) and *Wife* (1975) were brought out and they address themselves to the trauma of an uprooted identity. While her first protagonist Tara Banerjee is a modest Bengali girl raised under traditional taboos, Dimple of *Wife* is more adventurous and energetic in responding to her situation.

The chapter four titled The Phase of Transition is devoted to the two story collections which were brought out in eighties. The stories collected in *Darkness* have a pathetic note in that they expose the atrocities heaped on immigrants in Canada. They present a very dismal picture of human life and most of the characters have been drawn as puppets, innocent victims of racial discrimination. That the Canadian experience proved the turning point in Mukherjee's personal life as well, lends these stories a tone of authenticity. The stories included in *The Middleman and Other Stories* were mostly written in United States and they grapple with the quality of experience in American milieu. These stories evoke less pathos and express no apparent animus against the American social system. They concentrate on the nature of individual experience when two culturally divergent characters confront each other to establish a rapport.

The fifth chapter centres round Mukherjee's recent phase termed Immigration and discusses *Jasmine*, *The Holder of the World* and *Leave It to Me*. Mukherjee's *magnum opus Jasmine* is a story of a fearless girl who crosses one hurdle after the other and never submits herself to the onslaughts of circumstances. Even in the most trying moment of sexual assault, she exhibits a rare inner strength, keeps up her poise and finally kills the wrong-doer. Entrapped in a situation of alarming proportions she moves ahead with extraordinary confidence and conviction. Mukherjee shows a rare gift of fictionalising history in *The Holder of the World* where two 17th century divergently opposed cultures meet and look for a correspondence between each other. In her latest work *Leave It to Me* Mukherjee reverts to her overriding pre-occupation with immigrant's theme and takes up other aspects of this complex phenomenon.

The quality of cultural conflict in all its multiplicity forms the crux of Bharati Mukherjee's accomplishments dealt with in the concluding chapter. It also takes into account the ingredients of her creative style punctuated with irony and understatement which arm her with an objectivity of outlook and approach. The unmistakable impression that finally emerges after a careful study of her works is one of affirmation of life and also of an inbuilt urge to live it on one's own terms. Bharati Mukherjee has an esteemed place in the luminous galaxy of Indian authors writing abroad with native ethos providing them a living ambience.

NAGENDRA KUMAR

ACKNOWLEDGEMENTS

I Sincerely acknowledge my indebtedness to my revered *Guru*, Dr. Surya Nath Pandey, Professor of English, Banaras Hindu University for everything that I learnt from him. It is also my privilege to recall the encouragements received from Prof. B.B. Singh, Head of the Department of English, Veer Kunwar Singh University, Arrah by sparing me from teaching assignment whenever it was imperative. I am equally beholden to Prof. B.N. Singh, Head of English Department, Arunachal University Itanagar for his competent advice from time to time. I also express my deep sense of obeisance to my dear parents and family members for their countless blessings. My younger brothers Upendra and Shailendra deserve my affectionate wishes for extending moral support during the preparation of this volume.

NAGENDRA KUMAR

CONTENTS

1

Introduction

Cross-cultural confrontation has received a pronounced impetus since the emergence of the Modernist movement in the very opening of the twentieth century. The Post-colonial discourse has also, among other things, addressed itself to analysing its intriguing ramifications. The globalisation of world economy can be looked upon as a natural offshoot of multiculturalism and intercultural interaction. In ancient times, the Western culture was practically confined to a certain territory and likewise, the Eastern culture had also a limited area to flourish with hardly any possiblity of mutual exchange between them. With the passage of time, many adventurous explorers from the West started discovering new wonders and the Indian culture and civilization was one of their findings. With further advancement men started putting on wings and flying to the far-off regions. This coming together meant enhanced interaction and mutual co-operation between nations in the field of industry, technology, information and education. Now many sporting events are being organised every year in one part of the world or the other partly to encourage inter-cultural and inter-racial awareness. Every culture has its own peculiarities and predilections which evoke a mixed response in one from a different cultural milieu. People quite often try their best to forge a workable synthesis between their native culture and that of the new set-up. This process is not a smooth one and it, more often than not, results in some psychological eccentricities alien to both the cultures. We can linger awhile to discuss what culture really means and to what extent it is impervious or vulnerable.

'Culture' is too vast and baffling a term to be precisely defined in a few pages. Several sociologists, anthropologists, historians and men of letters have tried to define culture from time to time. However, the most comprehensive interpretation comes from T.S. Eliot, one of the propounders of the Modernist movement. Even he seems to be diffident and calls his treatise *Notes Towards the Definition of Culture*. In the first paragraph of its 'Introduction,' Eliot makes his aim clear, "My aim is to help to define a word, the word *culture*."[1] He initiates his discussion on culture and its ingredients with a simple proposition — "Culture may even be described simply as that which makes life worth living" (*Notes*, p. 27). Thus, Eliot sees culture as the way of life, as one which affects us and is affected, in turn, by our activities. He believes that culture is ideally a whole way of life, lived commonly and variously by a whole people. N.A. Nikam in his attempt to define culture, quotes a translated verse from *Kathopanisad* : "In the quest of the imperishable (the good) that one chooses is his." Thus, culture, according to him, "is a quest for good but it is not good if the quest is not free choice. The quest and the choice are, therefore, the two ingredients of culture, and the tradition is formed by the culmination of centuries of history, or a tradition may be defined as a 'passage' in which there is both persistence and renewal. So, cultural concepts are both ancient and contemporary, traditional as well as modern."[2]

It is a common tendency to confuse culture with civilization. Civilization has a reference to an advanced state of society judged on the basis of its culture, science, industry, laws, government, wars, transport and communication, architecture and planning of cities. Culture concerns only the intellectual and human side of all this achievement. Civilization pertains to the entire population of a country or nation while the culture is concern of chosen few who are enlightened and civilization may sometimes act against culture. That is why Eliot categories culture of a society in two as higher and lower depending upon the educational accomplishments of its members. To quote him,

> Now there are of course higher cultures and lower cultures, and the higher cultures in general are distinguished by differentiation of function, so that you can speak of the less cultured and the more cultured

> strata of society, and finally, you can speak of individuals as being exceptionally cultured (*Notes*, p. 120).

Eliot believes that there is a very close relationship between culture and religion. It is religion of a people which makes them culturally different from the people of other faiths. Two religions may have something in common but their differences might bring about a clash among their followers. It is really very difficult to reconcile between two antagonistic religions. Eliot begins his enquiry into the relationship between culture and religion with a very important assertion :

> No culture has appeared or developed except together with religion ... culture will appear to be the product of religion, or the religion the product of the culture (*Notes*, p. 15).

While discussing culture and religion, Eliot tries to avoid the two alternative errors of treating religion and culture as two separate things between which there is a relation and of identifying religion with culture. He regards culture of a people 'as an *incarnation* of its religion' for want of a better term to avoid misconception likely to be caused by the words 'relation' and 'identification.' To cite him :

> The truth, partial truth, or falsity of a religion neither consists in the cultural achievements of the peoples professing that religion, nor submits to being exactly tested by them (*Notes*, p. 33).

Eliot thinks that a people whose culture has been formed together with a religion of partial truth, may live that religion with greater fidelity than those whose culture is the product of a truer light. To consider one's culture as significant enjoins upon the claimant to see whether his society fully conforms to the values of his religious conviction. Eliot thinks that religion is indispensable for culture :

> Any religion ... gives an apparent meaning to life, provides the framework for a culture, and protects the mass of humanity from boredom and despair (*Notes*, p. 34).

It is, thus, apparent that culture owes much of its existence to religion. An individual, class or group or a society's way of living is moulded and shaped by its religion which in turn becomes the religion of that particular society. In other words, we can say that culture and religion are complementary to each other. Viewing the deep affinity between them, Eliot dilates :

> And both 'religion' and 'culture,' besides meaning different things from each other, should mean for the individual and for the group something towards which they strive, not merely something which they possess. Yet there is an aspect in which we can see a religion as the whole way of life of a people, from birth to the grave, from morning to night and even in sleep, and that way of life is also its culture (*Notes*, p. 31).

Though religion forms a sound basis of a culture, in actual life, culture and religion are not so completely unified. Although "what is part of our culture is also a part of our lived religion," the fact remains that "the actual religion of no European people has ever been purely Christian..." (*Notes*, p. 31). Bits and traces of more primitive faiths have been more or less absorbed. That means, there is no identification between culture and the true religion at its purest. But they should not also be regarded as two separate things between which there is only a relation. Eliot takes an idealistic view of both culture and religion. As he affirms :

> It is only when we imagine our culture as it ought to be, if our society were a really Christian society, that we can dare to speak of Christian culture as the highest culture; it is only by referring to all the phases of this culture, which has been the culture of Europe, that we can affirm that it is the highest culture that the world has ever known (*Notes*, p. 33).

Eliot finds that both democracy and liberalism, as political or social philosophies, have lost their cogency for behaviour. Moreover, they can be exploited and distorted by totalitarian states. A compromise between the theory of the state and the tradition of society was brought about in Fascist Italy. This country was still agricultural and Catholic. In a more highly industrialised country in Western Europe, like Britain, the materialistic philosophy might flourish more easily and outrageously. "And the tendency of unlimited materialism," writes Eliot, "is to create bodies of men and women — of all classes — detached from tradition, alienated from religion, and susceptible to mass suggestion : in other words, a mob. And a mob will be no less a mob if it is well fed, well clothed, well housed, and well disciplined."[3] Eliot, thus rejects the liberal notion that religion is a matter of private belief and of conduct in private life as untenable. However, the majority of Christians \are not conscious of the moral and cultural dilemma presented by the modern materialistic civilisation.

However, the existence of culture is still commonly assumed, but it is supposed to be the property of a small section of society. This assumption naturally and usually leads to two conclusions. First, 'Culture can only be the concern of a small minority, and that there is no place for it in the society of the future.' Second, 'in the society of the future the culture which has been the possession of the few must be put at the disposal of every body' (Eliot, 1948 1 : 33). Eliot finds a parallel to this so-called democratic attitude towards culture in the Puritan antipathy to monasticism and the ascetic life and in the condemnation by the extreme Protestantism of the enclosed and contemplative life.

This attitude to culture is not correct. Even among the primitive societies, there can be discerned differentiations of function amongst the members of the higher types, which naturally result in the formation of levels of culture in a given society. At a higher stage of society, some functions are more honoured than others, and this division leads to the development of classes, in which 'higher honour and higher privilege are accorded, not merely to the person as functionary but as member of the class' (Eliot, 1948, 1 : 35). But the class itself presupposes the function of maintaining the part of the total culture which pertains to that class. In a healthy society this maintenance of a particular level of culture is 'to the benefit, not merely of the class which maintains it, but of the society as a whole' (Eliot, 1948, 1 : 35). As such, it should not be supposed that the culture of a higher class is superfluous either to the society as a whole or to the majority. Therefore, it would be wrong to press the equalitarian principle for the culture of the higher class to be shared equally by all other classes. However, the survival of the culture of the higher class is dependent upon the health of the culture of the people in general and as a whole.

Eliot uses the term 'culture' in three senses. As he holds in the beginning of the very first chapter of *Notes* :

> The term culture has different associations according to whether we have in mind the development of an individual, of a group or class, or of a whole society (*Notes*, p. 21).

Thus he maintains that there are three ways of regarding culture : as the culture of the individual, as the culture of a group or class, or as the culture of a whole society. Envisaging an interdependence among these three orbits of culture, Eliot is of the view that :

> The culture of the individual is dependent upon the culture of a group or class, and that the culture of the group or class is dependent upon the culture of the whole society to which that group or class belongs. Therefore, it is the culture of the society that is fundamental (*Notes*, p. 21).

However, the difference between the three applications of the term, culture 'can be best apprehended by asking how far, in relation to the individual, the group, and society as a whole, the conscious aim to achieve culture has any meaning.' Eliot believes that a good deal of confusion could be avoided, if we refrained from setting before the group, what can be the aim only of the individual; and before society as a whole what can be the aim only of a group. Eliot points out that, usually, the men of letters and moralists have discussed culture only in the first two senses, especially the first, without relation to the third. For example, Matthew Arnold in *Culture* and *Anarchy*, is primarily concerned with the 'perfection of an individual. But T.S. Eliot examines culture in relation to the whole society, first.

The importance of the social background for a complete picture of culture can be ascertained by a consideration of the several kinds of attainments to be had in different contexts. First, by culture we may mean 'refinement of manners — or urbanity and civility.' Second, we may be thinking of 'learning and a close acquaintance with the accumulated wisdom of the past.' Third, culture may imply 'philosophy in the widest sense — an interest in, and some ability to manipulate abstract ideas.' Fourth, 'the art' also may well be implied (*Notes*, pp. 22-23). All these attainments of culture are usually taken piecemeal, and 'what we seldom have in mind in all of these things at the same time.' But if we look at the several activities of culture just listed, we must conclude that no perfection in any one of them, to the exclusion of the others, can confer culture on anybody. As such 'the person who contributes to culture, however important his contribution may be, is not always a cultured person' (*Notes*, p. 23). It is so because, we know that good manners, without education, intellect or sensibility to the arts, tend towards mere automatism; that learning without good manners or sensibility is pedantry; that intellectual ability without the more human attributes is admirable only in the same way as the brilliance of a chess child prodigy, and that the "arts without intellectual context are vanity" (*Notes*, p. 23). From this analysis and comparison of the constituents of culture, Eliot comes to the following conclusion :

> And if we do not find culture in any one of these perfections alone, so we must not expect any one person to be accomplished in all of them; we shall come to infer that the wholly cultured individual is a phantasm; and we shall look for culture, not in any one group of individuals, but more widely; and we are driven in the end to find it in the pattern of the society as a whole (*Notes*, p. 23).

However, this does not mean that there does not exist the culture of an individual, or of a group or class. What is meant is only that neither the culture of the individual can be isolated from that of the group nor the culture of the group can be abstracted from that of the whole society. 'Our notion of perfection must take all three senses of culture into account at once.' Then the various groups concerned with each activity of culture in a society, of whatever grade, should not be thought to be distinct and exclusive, "on the contrary, it is only by overlapping and sharing of interests, by participation and mutual appreciation, that the cohesion necessary for culture can (sic) obtain" (*Notes*, p. 24). This may be called an organic view of culture, as against the atomic one prevalent in modern times. Eliot is against any compartmentalisation of the cultural pursuits. This ideal of the integrity of culture is very closely related to Eliot's idea of a comprehensive tradition. As early as 1919, he had observed :

> I have tried to point out the importance of the relation of the poem to other poems by other authors, and suggested the conception of poetry as a living whole of all the poetry that has ever been written.[4]

This formulation about poetry, one of the arts constituting culture, very clearly anticipates the 'pattern of the society as a whole' as the total repository of culture.

Together with this comprehensiveness also goes a complexity of the cultural pattern, at a higher level of development. At a primitive stage of the society, the cultural functions are simple and as such, easily combined by certain individuals. But, with the growth of the society, the functions are expanded and differentiated. This process of development leads to specialization, which ultimately creates classes. "As a society develops," writes Eliot, "towards functional complexity and differentiation, we may expect the emergence of several cultural levels : in short, the culture of the class or group will present itself" (*Notes*, p. 25). Then there takes place a struggle or rivalry between the diverse classes or groups, either for autonomy or dominance. A conflict and competition ensues. The tension in the society may also show itself in a tension within the mind of the more conscious individual. However, this friction may at some stages and in some situations be highly creative, though it is to be investigated whether it is the result or cause of the increased consciousness thus engendered.

Eliot also dwells on several channels for the transmission of culture. Culture, as distinguishable from knowledge about culture, is picked up in various trades and crafts. An apprentice learns not only the skills but an entire way of life. The universities impart a sort of culture even to such alumni who are not interested in education. The societies of the masonic type initiate their members into a particular style of living :

> But by far the most important channel of transmission of culture remains the family : and when family life fails to play its part, we must expect our culture to deteriorate (*Notes*, p. 43).

The family is the primary channel of cultural transmission. No man wholly escapes from the kind, or wholly surpasses the degree, of culture which he acquired from his early environment.

Language is also of utmost importance in the growth and development of a culture. The cultural standard of an individual, of a group or class, or of a society depends upon the use of their language, which is moulded and shaped by the educational status. Like religion which plays an important role in shaping a culture, language serves the purpose of stratification of a culture based upon the education. Even environment is of no less importance than language and education in the determination of a culture. A culture owes very deep to the environment from which it gets its nourishment and life. It provides the base for cultural formation and its growth and in the absence of it, the proper growth of culture might be affected. In the case of an individual family stands for environment, in the case of a class or group or society, locality signifies environment.

Eliot also talks of the idea of 'constellation' and 'Satellite' culture, simply because in England there exists atleast a national culture which has some affinity (religious, linguistic, racial and cultural) with the culture of the different class or group of that nation. These things common among the culture of individual group or society open the gate for the formation of national culture to which Eliot refers as 'Constellation,' a product of different satellite cultures. We can put this idea in another way — if we consider national culture as a 'language' and the culture of different groups or societies of that nation which ultimately forms the national culture, as 'dialect,' then we find that different dialects of that particular language have to some extent certain qualities common to that language which bind and unite them with that language. In fact, Eliot has expressed this view for the unity and integrity of Europe. In Eliot's opinion almost all European countries have something in common, rituals and ceremonies of religion, words, structure, idiom, intonation and rhythm of language, and racial affinity, in common among themselves. That's why despite the differences among them they have some common traits which is the reason behind the unity of Europe to which Eliot expresses as 'unity' and 'diversity.' Eliot's concept of 'constellation' and 'satellite' culture has a broader function to fulfil, his dream of unity of European continent.

Raymond Williams, another critic known for his cultural obsessions, finds fault with Eliot's concept of culture for its ignoring "the economic factor."[5] Eliot's suppression of the relation between culture and politics has also been noted by the eminent critic as a major flaw in his thinking. It should not, however, create the impression that the two critics are diametrically opposed to each other in their appreciations of the term culture and its bewildering dimensions. Eliot's idea of a national culture to be a constellation of satellite cultures is very close to Williams's idea of a series of related complex developments. In fact, Williams's objections are rooted in the static quality of Eliot's idea of a common culture to which he has devoted a full chapter in his seminal book *Culture and Society*. Another perceptive critic Terry Eagleton has meticulously compared the two contestants of culture in a perspicuous way. Since his comments underline various shreds of culture, they can be profitably reproduced verbatim :

> Both Eliot and Williams are concerned to contrast a *common* with a *uniform* culture; both stress the unevenness and variety of any lived common experience. But for Eliot the unevenness springs ironically from a quite rigid structure of levels : all will not experience alike because all will not participate alike. Williams, while agreeing that full participation by one individual in the whole culture will be impossible, locates the essential variety of development in the culture's content, rather than simply in its form; a culture will reveal the unevenness of any process of growth which engages the activity of a great number of men, but it is the variety of what is created, rather than the levels of conscious creation which is seen as primary.[6]

The foregoing interpretation of the term culture and its components demonstrates that there is absolutely no possibility of reaching at a uniform tangible pattern in this respect. Diversity of cultural assumptions and complications provides little scope for total assimilation. In cases where cultural dissimilarities are much sharper in terms of ethnic, racial, linguistic and religious determinants, the issue gets irredeemably complex for the immigrant to cope with.

Nowadays the problem of migration is different from that of the pre-historic and early times. Today people are leaving their countries willingly under certain motives for the satisfaction of some personal ambitions. But in early times it was not migration at all, it was the transportation of third world people as labourer to a slave island. That is why today people migrate only with "a part of the total culture in which so long as they remained at home, they participated" (*Notes*, p. 64). Therefore, their adjustment in a different social, religious, economic and political milieu is not so pathetic as was that of the early emigres, because of the former's education and determination. In early times, people were more or less illiterate and their illiteracy was the reason behind their nostalgia (their adherence to mother country's religion, culture and language). In early times, it was whole tribe or atleast a wholly representative part of it that moved together. Therefore it was a total culture that moved away. This shows their outer-migration because their inner world is occupied by their mother country. This outer migration of different races and communities creates racial, cultural and linguistic confusion and this becomes a great hurdle in the formation of a national culture. The new culture which develops in this island is bafflingly alike and also different from the parent culture because as the time passes, the old values gradually diminish leaving their remnants in their memories while the migration in modern times is entirely otherwise.

No doubt, America is the 'crowning glory' of our time and so it has become a sole dream of people around the world. The young ambitious personnel, especially from third world countries where they cannot get enough to do, are making an unabated flow to America. This flow of divergent races, classes and cultures has totally changed the face of America. These aspirants to the New World are dead set even in their own country to blindly imitate American habits and American culture. They feel more American than their native counterparts in all respects and obviously their cultural elasticity enables them adjust to the new set up comfortably. But it is rarely so that everyone who goes to America finds the same amicable environment. Some people are lucky enough to get their dreams fulfilled while others become victims of circumstances and are forced to lead worse lives than the ones they left behind. Those who experience acculturation sing with America and are never tired of showering all praise on the country of their adoption for its 'providence,' but others can never forget that plunge into a culturally different ethos has been a 'big mistake' for them. No doubt, cultural conflict has minimised in modern times because people have become primary and all other things have become secondary. The finesse of culture has lost its lustre in the dazzling light of American discotheque. Madona and Michael Jackson have obscured the chanting of *Ramayana* and *The Gita*.

In fact, the class which moves out of its cultural contours, has no love lost for its mother land. Moreover, there is so much of cultural mixing in the post-colonial era that it has given birth to 'hybrid-culture.' In every country the highest class (and especially in India) is worse affected by this phenomenon. As Ashcroft and his colleagues observe :

> Post-colonial culture is inevitably a hybrid phenomenon involving a dialectical relationship between the grafted European cultural systems and an indigenous ontology, with its impulse to create or recreate an independent local identity. Such construction or reconstruction occurs as a dynamic interaction between European hegemonic and 'peripheral' subversions of them.[7]

The contemporary times have witnessed a total transformation of cultural logic in that they have almost done away with all possibilities of nursing the old specific sense of culture. Earlier it was religion which was more vital, to use the Wordsworthian phrase 'the breath and finer spirit' of culture. Now it is economy which is governing supreme in the formation and alteration of cultural norms of a society. Fredric Jameson rightly comments :

> The post modern is...the forcefield in which very different kinds of cultural impulses — what Raymond Williams has usefully termed 'residual' and "emergent" forms of cultural production must make their way. If we do not achieve some general sense of a cultural dominant, then we fall back into a view of present history as sheer

> heterogeneity, random difference, a coexistence of a host of distinct forces whose affectivity is undecidable.[8]

This new capitalistic culture which has emerged in post-modern times is an outcome of American dominance as Jameson convincingly puts it :

> Post modern culture is the internal and superstructural expression of a whole new wave of American military and economic domination throughout the World : in this sense, as throughout class history, the underside of culture is blood, torture, death and terror.[9]

The process of migration to America that started in mid-nineteenth century has reached a new high in terms of immigrant population within a span of one hundred years. People from all over the world are drawn towards this country for a variety of reasons. Notwithstanding their intention, those who choose to stay on and finally settle down, experience qualitative cultural transformation, which with men of letters gets appropriated in their works. Bharati Mukherjee's creative world best manifests immigrant experience which can be advantageously analysed in the light of the making of her artist to be discussed in the chapter that follows.

REFERENCES

1. T.S. Eliot, *Notes Towards the Definition of Culture* (London : Faber, 1948, rptd. 1962), p. 13. Unless otherwise indicated all citations refer to this edition.
2. N.A. Nikam, *Some Concepts of Indian Culture* (Shimla : Indian Institute of Advanced Studies, 1973), pp. 1-2.
3. T.S. Eliot, *The Idea of a Christian Society* (London : Faber, 1939; rptd. 1948), p. 21.
4. T.s. Eliot, "Tradition and Individual Talent," *Selected Essays* (London : Faber, 1932), p. 17.
5. Raymond Williams, *Culture and Society* (London : Penguin, 1958), p. 236.
6. Terry Eagleton, "Eliot and a Common Culture" in Graham Martin, ed. *Eliot in Perspective* (London : Macmillan, 1970), p. 286.
7. Bill Ashcroft, Gareth Griffiths and Helen Tiffin, *The Empire Writers Back* (London : Routledge, 1989), p. 195.
8. Fredric Jameson, *Post-Modernism or The Cultural Logic of Late Capitalism* (London : Versov, 1991), p. 6.
9. *Ibid*, p. 5.

2

The Shaping of Creative Sensibility

Bharati Mukherjee, an India-born American novelist has received considerable critical attention from almost all the quarters of the globe in a relatively short period of just twenty five years. She has been widely acknowledged as a 'voice' of expatriate-immigrant sensibility. The biographical details of her life and the major formative impacts on her sensibility will engage our attention in the following pages.

I

Bharati Mukherjee was born on 27 July 1940, in a Bengali Brahmin family of Calcutta. Her father Sudhir Lal Mukherjee was a pharmaceutical chemist and her mother, Bina Banejee Mukherjee was a housewife. She spent her first eight years as a member of a large extended family. Shortly after India gained Independence, she lived with her parents and two sisters in London for about three years, where she became fluent in English. In 1951 the family returned to Calcutta and Mukherjee joined the English-speaking Loreto Convent School, run by Irish nuns. She lived with her parents in fairly comfortable circumstances since her father was a co-owner of pharmaceutical factory. Theirs was a spacious house tastefully furnished with furniture and artefacts quite typical of the post-Independence era. There were rolltop desks, Victorian love seats, carved tea-tables and ornate lamps. Adapting to the hot and humid climate of Calcutta was a modified colonial architecture sporting shuttered green windows and gargoyle-headed storm water drains. Inside, some rooms replicated decorations from English housekeeping magazines, but again, an Indianness was noticeable in the framed portraits of ancestors reverentially mounted on the walls of the drawing room or study. On special days of rememberance, Hindu rituals used to obscure the western artefacts-garlanded portraits, flickering brass lamps, 'alpana' on the floors, banana leaves strung along the doorways.

In view of her privileged childhood, Mukherjee and her sisters were chauffeured to the convent school. Quite characteristic of this class of Bengalis, the family was 'westernized' in the sense that English education was valued, and much literature, philosophy, social principles got transmitted through the language. However, in more intimate convictions, the family observed Hindu practices and beliefs. In 1958, Mukherjee's father lost his partnership in the factory and moved his family to Baroda, where he joined the Research and Development wing of a large Bombay complex. In the meantime, Bharati Mukherjee completed her B.A. (Honours) in English at the University of Calcutta in 1959. Subsequently, she took her M.A. degree in English from the University of Baroda in 1961.

Sensing his daughter's aptitude for creative work, Mr. Mukherjee encouraged her to join Creative Writing Programme in the United States. She went to the University of Iowa's Writers' Workshop with a P.E.O. International Peace Scholarship where she obtained an MFA in creative writing in 1963 and a Ph.D. in English and Comparative Literature in 1969. It was during her stint at the University of Iowa that Mukherjee met Clark Blaise, the Canadian novelist, Professor and journalist and married him in North American style one lunch hour in September 1963. In 1966 the couple moved to Canada and lived there as Canadian citizens till 1980, first in Toronto, then in Montreal, a period that Mukherjee looks back with pain and anger. However, the couple took a bold decision to move to U.S.A. in 1980 and since then they have been living there as U.S. citizens.

After moving to Canada and before settling down finally at the University of California, Berkeley, where presently she is a Professor of English, Mukherjee had worked on several teaching assignments. First she took the job of instructor in English at Marquette University, Milwaukee, Wisconsin during 1964-65 session followed by a similar appointment at Madison in 1965. She worked as a lecturer in McGill University, Montreal, Quebec from 1966 to1969, where she was elevated to assistant professorship in 1969 and to associate professorship in 1973. Thereafter, she joined Skidmore College, Saratoga Springs, New York as Professor of English in 1979. She also taught at Queens College, New York for a brief period before finally joining the present assignment at Berkeley.

Bharati Mukherjee's academic and professional career won him many a laurel. Twice she availed herself of Grants from McGill University in 1968 and 1970 besides winning Canada Arts Council Grant twice in the years 1973-74 and 1977. She was also awarded the prestigious Shastri-Indo-Canadian Institute Grant during the year 1976-77. She was a recipient of Guggenheim Foundation Award in 1978-79, and Canadian Government Award in 1982. She also won the first prize from Periodical Distribution Association in 1980 for her short story "Isolated Incidents." Mukherjee has also been honoured with the National Book Critics Circle Award, for her short stories collection, *The Middleman and Other Stories* in 1989. Her creative *oeuvre* comprises five novels — *The Tiger's Daughter* (1972), *Wife* (1975), *Jasmine* (1989), *The Holder of the World* (1993) and *Leave It to Me* (1997) — and two collections of short, stories — *Darkness* (1985) and *The Middleman and Other Stories* (1988). She has also co-authored with her husband two non-fictional works.

II

Like the eponymous narrator of her novel *Jasmine*, Bharati Mukherjee has changed citizenships and lived in various cultural milieus with disorienting rapidity. During her odyssey as a writer for almost three decades her creative sensibility has undergone many changes. There has been an 'on-going quest' from 'expatriation to immigration' in her writings. Her major concern as a writer has been the life of South-Asian expatriates/immigrants in U.S.A. and Canada and the problem of 'Acculturation' and 'Assimilation'. An examination of the works of Mukherjee reveals a movement from expatriation to immigration. This movement coincides with her immigration from Canada to U.S.A. Mukherjee's interpretation of and reaction to her experience in Canada led her to see herself as an expatriate and this theme of expatriation is reflected in her writings in Canada. In the U.S.A. there is a growing recognition of herself as an immigrant with an increasingly strong attachment to America and this experience of immigration is reflected in her writings in the U.S.A.

Before discussing Bharati Mukherjee's tryst with the problems of expatriation and immigration it is of foremost importance to linger awhile on certain terms closely associated with expatriate sensibility. While the main thrust of expatriation is on the native country and traditions left behind, immigration lays all emphasis on the cultural life of the host country. The expatriate dwells on his "ex" status of the past, while the immigrant celebrates his present in the new country.

Expatriation is quite a widespread phenomenon in this century and George Steiner describes the expatriate writer as "the contemporary everyman."[1] Uma Parameswaran considers the phrase "the expatriate sensibility" as a legitimate literary term in the context of today's Commonwealth Literature.[2] Christine Gomez gives a still more perceptive definition of the term 'expatriation' :

> Expatriation is actually a complex state of mind and emotion which includes a wistful longing for the past, often symbolised by the ancestral home, the pain of exile and homelessness, the struggle to maintain the difference between oneself and the new, unfriendly surroundings, an assumption of moral and cultural superiority over the host country and a refusal to accept the identity forced on one by the environment. The expatriate builds a cocoon around herself/himself as a refuse from cultural dilemmas and from the experienced hostility or unfriendliness in the new country.[3]

Faced with rejection, the new comer clings to his ethnic identity. As Viney Kirpal observes, "Revival of ethnicity makes bearable to some extent the marginal shadowy existence of these migrants in the new land."[4]

Bharati Mukherjee admits of being subjected to racial discrimination in Canada. While her husband's creative acumen was recognised, her potentialities went ignored and unresponded to. Canada's hostility to Indians and the non-recognition of her writing in Canada are the twin recurring themes which appear with almost obsessive regularity in Mukherjee's early works. She experienced herself as 'a psychological expatriate' in Canada and clung to her ethnic identity" — I remember how bracing it was to cloak myself in my own Brahminical elegance."[5] She became a Civil Rights activist in Canada and wrote about the crippling effect of racism on individuals. Not only in the personal and political writings of Mukherjee but also in her canadian fiction, the experience of expatriation is poignantly manifested. Life in Canada — fourteen years of it — tested her spirit to the breaking point. Her essay "Invisible Woman" is a blistering reflection on those years. She writes : "Many including myself left (Canada) unable to keep our twin halves together."[6]

Viewing herself as a writer with two novels to her credit, Bharati Mukherjee identified V.S. Naipaul as her model in 1977. In *Days and Nights in Calcutta,* she says :

> In myself I detect a pale and immature reflection of Naipaul; it is he who has written most movingly about the pain and absurdity of art and exile, of 'third world art' and exile among the former colonizers; the tolerant incomprehension of hosts, the absolute impossibility of ever having a home, a 'desh'.[7]

Identification with Naipaul at this stage evidences that Mukherjee treated herself as an expatriate writer on the basis of her first two novels.

The process of change from expatriation to immigration got off during Mukherjee's stay in India in 1973-74. She recalls, "The year in India had forced me to view myself more as an immigrant than an exile."[8] The realization of fluid identities and alternate realities too could be traced to this sojourn in India as she further observes :

> In India, different perceptions of reality converge without embarrassing anyone. My fear in India had shown me that I did not need to discard my western education in order to retrieve the dim shape of my Indian one.

The years between *The Tiger's Daughter*, and *Darkness* mark a change in the inner world of Bharati Mukherjee. In 1985, distancing herself from the earlier stance of an expatriate, she emphatically voices the futility of such a stance. In the Introduction to *Darkness*, she says that until the Spring of 1984, "I had thought of myself, inspite of a white husband and two assimilated sons as an expatriate."[9] She defines expatriates as conscious knowers of their fate and immigrants — in particular to Canada — as "lost souls bet upon and pathetic." In respect of the stylistic devices of an expatriate writer, she referred to irony, so tellingly employed by Naipaul :

> Like V.S. Naipaul, in whom I imagined a model, I tried to explore state-of-the-art expatriation. Like Naipaul, I used a mordant and self-protective irony in describing my character's pain. Irony promised both detachment from, and superiority over, those well-bred post-colonials much like myself, adrift in the new world, wondering if they would ever belong.[10]

Thus, 1984 is a turning point in Mukherjee's sensibility and style. She says "The Book I dream of updating is no longer *A Passage to India*, it is *Call It Sleep*." She thus reveals that she is freed of the debility of expatriate nostalgia by the stringencies of life in the New World. What frees her from the company of persons who surrender "little bits of a reluctant self every year clutching the souvenirs of an ever-retreating past?" The stories collected in *Darkness* mark a distinct departure in that Mukherjee is no longer an aloof expatriate writer. Now onwards, she regards expatriation as a restrictive and self-defeating attitude in a writer. The expatriate writer nurses his grievances, parades his pain of exile and becomes a "permanent scold." Ultimately this adversely affects his sensibility and his writing becomes self-imitative and predictable.

In the U.S.A. Bharati Mukherjee sees herself as an immigrant writer. In her works which were either completed or fully written here she explores the immigrant sensibility, recognizing its duality and flexible identity besides taking into cognizance alternate realities. In the Introduction to *Darkness* she lays bare her position and creative priorities :

> The transformation as writer and as resident of the new world, occurred with the act of immigration to the U.S.A.... For me it is a movement away from the aloofness

> of expatriation, to the exuberance of immigration (pp. 2-3).

The movement from expatriation to immigration is also reflected in the choice of the writers who shaped Mukherjee's creative sensibility. After outgrowing and discarding the posture of an expatriate she rejected Naipaul as a model and chose Bernard Malamud whose central concern was the life of minorities and its agonies. Though partially influenced by Isaac Babel, Conrad and Chekhov, she followed Malamud as his writings instilled unusual confidence in her :

> Like Malamud, I write about a minority community which escapes the ghetto and adapts itself to the patterns of the dominant American culture. Like Malamud's my work seems to find quite naturally a moral center. Isaac Babel is another author who is a literary ancestor for me. I also feel a kinship with Joseph Conrad and Anton Chekhov. But Malamud most of all speaks to me as a writer and I admire his work a great deal. Immersing myself in his work gave me the self-confidence to write about my own community.[11]

Malamud taught Mukherjee how to overcome being viewed as 'the Other' in a diagonally different cultural milieu. While Malamud's characters are from poor classes, humble shoe-makers, tailors and bakers, Mukherjee's immigrants are doctors, university professors, businessmen and women married to upwardly mobile professionals. Both address themselves to the diasporic experience of cultural alienation. Entering Malamud's literary space enabled Mukherjee to move her fiction from the constantly shifting margin to the unstable and shifting centre which has no fixed place. Both employ humour as a means of transcending one's fate in the face of chaos, displacement and alienation. While Malamud's characters retain their Yiddish accents and become only partly Americanized, many of Mukherjee's immigrants speak and act American. One of the reasons for Mukherjee's adoption of Malamud as a literary mentor can be seen as a strategy to place herself in the working class Jewish tradition and thus to lend authenticity to her delineation of her socially, if not always economically, marginal characters. The immigrant characters of both the authors dream Westward, specially to California, the furthest geographical distance from their Eastern roots, where possibly they can re-shape their lives. It was this indebtedness to Malamud that prompted Mukherjee to dedicate her first collection of stories *Darkness* to the great Jewish writer. It should, however, not be construed that Mukherjee's fiction is slavishly imitative of Malamud in character. In the same interview she explains her fundamental dissimilarities with Malamud's vision :

> I was born into a Hindu Bengali Brahmin family which means I have a different sense of self, of existence, and of mortality, than do writers like Malamud. I believe that our souls can be reborn in another body, so the perspective I have about a single character's life is different from that of an American writer who believes that he has only one life.

Thus, Mukherjee's approach to life and its problems is deeply moored in her Indian upbringing. Maya Manju Sharma refers to this aspect of her creative personality :

> In her fiction Mukherjee handles Western themes and settings as well as characters who are westernized or bicultural. Yet she is forced to admit that the very structure of her imagination is essentially Hindu, and essentially moral.[12]

In Alison interview she draws the demarcating line also between Naipaul and herself as writers of the third world countries :

> V.S. Naipaul...writes about living in perpetual exile and the impossibility of ever having a home. Like Naipaul, I am a writer from the third world but unlike him I left India by choice to settle in the U.S. I have adopted this country as my home. I view myself as an American author in the tradition of other American authors whose ancestors arrived at Ellis Island.

Having ascertained her affinity with American authors, Mukherjee spells her aim, "My task as an author is to make my intricate and unknown world comprehensible to mainstream American readers." She considers herself as the repository and exponent of the experiences rendered by immigration. Through a review of her own several transitions, she has evolved a credo for the new immigrant voices, which she calls "Maximalism." This she claims, is the key to introducing diversity to America's fairly stagnant "Minimalist fiction" of "mainstream," "collective dread" and common cause. Her attack is levelled at writers such as Updike and Cheever. According to Mukherjee, Earnest Hemingway and William Faulkner gained some kind of international readership. The later writers promoted by market place hype were those who pretended to speak for America but used only limited categories of subjects like Vietnam, "dead end jobs and midlife crises." Their tepid fiction and timid refusal to take position against other currents within America caused a dullness to set into the literature of the '70s. "Minimalism" according to Mukherjee was a deft short hand for experience which was supposed typical but, in actuality, ignored major change America was passing through.

"An epic was washing up on its shores," says Mukherjee. The immigration offices provide the stage for the new drama. She sees immigrants who are confident, sophisticated, and poised, as ones who will not melt into an American mainstream but visibly expand the margins of what one may call "the American experience." These new Americans are neither nostalgic for their personal past nor afraid of the unfamiliar present. Their main strategy is adaptation without surrender. To honour their potential and vitality, Bharati Mukherjee formulates her "Maximalist" credo :

> I can imagine a poster over the United States Court House : WELCOME MAXIMALISTS, HELLO EXPANSIONISTS. The New America I know and have been living in for the last seven years is a world, by definition of doubles .... They have all shed past lives and languages, and have travelled half the world in every direction to come here and begin again. They are bursting with stories, too many to begin telling. They have lived through centuries of history in a single lifetime... Village born, colonized, traditionally raised, educated. What they have assimilated in 30 years has taken the West 10 times that number of years to create. Time travel is a reality .... I have seen it in my own life. Bionic men and women are living among us.[13]

Bharati Mukherjee is her own theorist and exemplar since her novels illustrate the credo of immigrant writing as a "Maximalist" act. Strenuously announcing and emphasising her American citizenship, she tends to downgrade her Indian heritage and affiliations. During her 1989 tour of India, she refused to answer questions about her "Indianness" several times. Yet the audience saw her sari-clad, dark-eyed, dark-haired, retaining an obvious Bengali-brahmin name, and heard her use Indian material in the extracts she read from her fiction. Malashri Lal aptly comments :

> Mukherjee has deliberately problematized her identity, perhaps over-reacting to the likelihood of being enclosed in a coterie culture geographically and ideologically separate from her chosen home and citizenship. One must allege here that her sense of Indianness is narrow, restrictive, somewhat bigoted, for no writer is characterised by his or her passport details. What matters is the literary material to which imagination is superimposed.[14]

The question before us is, how far is the Maximalist credo tenable? Mukherjee has shrugged off her own Indianness and claimed that her immigrants move away from their origins in India yet one can easily find the echoes of Indian English, Indian sensibility in her novels.

Actually, the problem of the credo lies with the maker of it. Bharati Mukherjee is seeking visible space in the American book market where it is more profitable to push the myth of Ellis Island than peddle the muck of Calcutta's Hooghly Docks. But a certain kind of "Indianness" is saleable. Mukherjee has made up a formula which apparently works — Indian characters in search of American citizenship retain sufficient Indianness to be exotic but float gleefully into American materialism. From this category of experience Mukherjee wishes to carve out her own speciality within the broader genre of American literature. In doing so, she underscores her repudiation of Indian culture and literary influence.

There are marked stages in the evolving creative vision of Bharati Mukherjee. With each passing year we encounter a more confident author, a more daring woman. Nothing happens automatically, nothing happens suddenly. There is always a deliberate and conscious effort on the part of the author contrived by the favourable circumstances. No doubt, that we encounter an entirely changed writer in *Darkness* but this dynamics of growth is present in *The Tiger's Daughter* and *Wife* also. In both these novels the author's voice is omniscient and irony her strategy. However, they are not written to imply, as Jasbir Jain says, "total rejection or a ruthless questioning of tradition or a love-hate relationship with the native heritage."[15] Rather, these early novels are travels in the 'psycho-social country' of self shared by many other Indians studying, living and working for long periods abroad in Europe or the United States.

Given Mukherjee's moral and metaphysical inclinations, it is all the more surprising that she should see herself as an immigrant American rather than an expatriate Indian. "Language gives me my identity," tells Mukherjee, "I am the writer I am because I write in North American English about immigrant in the New World."[16] Mukherjee's immigration is not so much her move from the Calcutta of the East to the Calcutta of the West (as she affectionately calls New York) by way of Canada, as it is her move from the English of Jane Austen to the American of Walt Whitman. She expresses her purpose in precise terms talking about the content of *Holder of the World* :

> I did not want *Holder of the World* to be a traditional historical novel, a period piece. I love history and I am fascinated by the handling of data, what is called information management. As the novel grew, draft by draft, I saw a way to bring these together... To me this was an experiment in virtual reality, a way of revising reliving history instead of rewriting it. I wanted to set up for American and Indian audiences how much Asia contributed to the notion of an American or European identity.[17]

According to Mukherjee, there are two kinds of writers — those who confirm what the public wants to know, and the other kind who disturb, interrogate the existing patterns. She clearly sees herself as belonging to the second variety. She tells Vrinda Nabar :

> Such writers are often misread. I sometimes think I've been too smart for my own good. I see a writer as always being in a minority of one, stating what is unsettling and disturbing. Knowledge and empathy have nothing to do with inherited race. A writer's identity is not exclusively biological : it is about the imagination claiming its territory and finding its own niche there.[18]

That Mukherjee is an autobiographical writer is the commonplace of critical literature on her. She pointed to her expanding vision to an interviewer :

> I have been wise enough to move away from particular autobiographical concerns — that my themes are larger, my strategies more complex.... Multiculturalism/diversity are key words for being American; they've also what I think are dramatising, injecting, 'quickening' my fiction.

Indian critics have invariably viewed Mukherjee's non-native concerns unfavourably. She explained her position to Jerry Pinto :

> I think my position has been misunderstood largely in India. I insist on being considered an American writer because I want America to realise that in the late 20th Century there can be no American Centre and periphery ... I am fighting the American establishment to be regarded as central. I want to destroy the whole notion that Asians, or people of a different colour are 'sojourners' whereas those who arrived in America from Germany or Sweden are 'settlers.' It's also a way of resisting exoticisation.

Knowing full well that she would have been more popular by grappling with Indian subjects and by playing down native values, she chose a different theme to ensure authenticity of experience :

> I could have been a greater success if I had stuck to Indian themes because that would have made it easy for the Establishment to slot me as an Indian writer. But I don't think one can live in America and work there and still write about an India that has changed while one has been away.

Mukherjee here alludes to a characteristic expatriate trait because the immigrants retain a fixed impression of their native country, an image formed at the time of departure. Naipaul's disenchantment with India can be interpreted in terms of the glorious image imprinted in his psyche by his grandparents. Naipaul, Malamud or others who served as literary models for Mukherjee, in various stages of her development could not suppress her innate artistic virtuosity. Bharati Mukherjee lived all these influences down and matured into a great writer by dint of her individual creative acumen which forms the content of the three substantive chapters that follow.

REFERENCES

1. George Steiner. *Extra-territorial : Papers on Language and Literature* (London : Faber, 1968), pp. 10-11.
2. Uma Parameswaran. "What Price Expatriation?" in Alastair Niven, ed. *The Commonwealth Writer Overseas : Themes of Exile andExpatriation* (Brussels : Libraire Marcel Didier, 1976), p. 41.
3. Christine Gomez. "The On-Going Quest of Bharati Mukherjee from Expatriation to Immigration" in R.K. Dhawan, ed. *Indian Women Novelists*, Vol. 3 (Delhi : Prestige, 1995), p. 72.
4. Viney Kirpal. *The Third-World Novel of Expatriation : A Study of Emigre Fiction by Indian, West African and Caribbean Writers* (New Delhi : Sterling, 1989), p. 165.
5. Bharati Mukherjee. "Immigrant Writing : Give Us Your Maximalists,!" *New York Times Book Review*, 28 August 1988, p. 28.
6. Bharati Mukherjee. "An Invisible Woman," *Saturday Night,* 96 (March 1981), 37.
7. Bhārati Mukherjee and Clark Blaise. *Days and Nights in Calcutta* (New York : Doubleday, 1977), p. 287.
8. *Ibid.*, p. 284.
9. Bharati Mukherjee. "Introduction", *Darkness* (Toronto : Penguin, 1985, Indian reprint 1990), p. 1.
10. *Ibid.*, p. 2.
11. Alison B. Carb. 'An Interview with Bharati Mukherjee,' *The Massachusetts Review*, Winter 1988-89, p. 650.
12. Maya Manju Sharma. "The Inner World of Bharati Mukherjee : From Expatriate to Immigrant." In Emmanuel S. Nelson, ed. *Bharati Mukherjee : Critical Perspectives* (New York, London : Garland Publishing, 1993), p. 18.

13. "Immigrant Writing : Give Us Your Maximalists," *New York Times Book Review*, 28 August 1988, p. 29.
14. Malashri Lal. "Bharati Mukherjee : The 'Maximalist' Credo," in K.N. Awasthi, ed. *Contemporary Indian English Fiction : An Anthology of Essays* (New Delhi : ABS Publications, 1993), pp. 57-58.
15. Jasbir Jain. "Foreignness of Spirit : The World of Bharati Mukherjee Novels," *Journal of Indian Writing in English*, 13, 2 (July 1985), p. 13.
16. Geoff Hancock. "An Interview with Bharati Mukheriee," *Canadian Fiction Magazine*, 59 (1987), 35.
17. Jerry Pinto. "Bharati but American," *The Sunday Times*, 5 January 1997, p. II.
18. Vrinda Nabar. "The Way I Write Has Changed Dramatically," *The Sunday Times*, 31 December 1995.

3

The Phase of Expatriation

Bharati Mukherjee's creative odyssey spans a period of about three decades which witnessed the publication of five novels and two story-collections, besides other non fictional writings. Mukherjee's creative world is inhabited by people of various religious faiths, diverse ethnicities and different cultural predilections so much so that it is almost a Noah's Ark. An instinctive urge to grapple with cultural tension best defines her creative impulse remarkably manifested in all her fictional writings. With a view to making an indepth study, her career can be conveniently divided in three well-marked stages as the phase of Expatriation (from 1972 to 1979), the phase of Transition (from 1980 to 1988), and the phase of Immigration (from 1989 onwards). The first phase that forms the content of third chapter comprises her two early novels *The Tiger's Daughter* (1972) and *Wife* (1975) which were written during her stay in Canada. The fourth chapter is devoted to the second phase of her development during which her two story collections *Darkness* (1985) and *The Middleman and Other Stories* (1988) were published. This was the transitional stage of her career when she moved to the United States in the beginning of 80's and was in the process of settling down in a new milieu. The third and recent phase, which is most prolific in terms of fictional output has been analysed in the fifth chapter. The three novels — *Jasmine* (1989), *The Holder of the World* (1993) and *Leave It to Me* (1997) — that were brought out during this period betray the resolution of earlier cultural tension since Mukherjee has experienced complete immigration in the American set up by now.

Bharati Mukherjee's first novel *The Tiger's Daughter* is a very fine manifestation of cultural conflict. This is an interesting study of an upper class Bengali Brahmin girl who goes to America for higher studies. Though afraid of the unknown ways of America in the beginning, she tries to adjust herself to it by entering into the wedlock with an American. She returns to India after seven years, only to find herself a total stranger in the inherited milieu. She realises that she is now neither Indian nor truly American. She is totally confused and lost.

The actual starting point of the story dates back to a rainy night in the year 1879. It was the day of the grand wedding ceremony of the daughters of Hari Lal Banerjee, the 'Zamindar' of Village Pachapara. Standing under a wedding canopy on the roof of his house Hari Lal Banerjee could have hardly imagined what future holds in store for his coming generations. He "did not hear the straining and imprisoned ghost of change."[1] Because

> the shadows of suicide or exile, of Bengali soil sectioned and ceded, of workers rising against their bosses could not have been divined by even a wise man in those days (p. 6).

After the marriage of Hari Lal Banerjee's daughters, life continued to be pleasant in the village Pachapara many more marriages took place and many deaths too. After two summers Hari Lal Banerjee fell a prey to an unseen assassin while mediating a feud. All the reputation and influence of Banerjee family died with him. Nobody knew at that time that "years later a young woman who had never been to Pachapara would grieve for the Banerjee family and try to analyse the reasons for its change. She would sit by a window in America to dream of Hari Lal, her great-grandfather, and she would wonder at the gulf that separated him from herself" (p. 9).

This young woman is nobody else but Tara Banerjee, the great grand daughter of Hari Lal Banerjee and the daughter of Bengal Tiger, the owner of famous Banerjee & Thomas (Tobacco) Co. Ltd. Tara is packed off by her father at an early age of fifteen for America for higher study. When this young Indian girl comes to terms with the American life her reactions are one of fear and anger :

> For Tara, Vassar had been an almost unsalvageable mistake. If she had not been a Banerjee, a Bengali Brahmin, the great grand daughter of Hari Lal Banerjee, or perhaps if she had not been trained by the good nuns at St. Blaise's to remain composed and ladylike in all emergencies, she would have rushed home to India at the end of her first week (p. 10).

In Poughkeepsie she feels homesick. She senses discrimination even if her room mate refuses to share her bottle of mango chutney. As it is typical of Indians who are proud of their family and genealogy, she defends her family and her country instinctively. At such moments when she thinks like breaking she even prays to goddess Kali for strength. When at the end of May, that first year abroad, girls around her prepare to go home she is seized by a vision of terror :

> She saw herself sleeping in a large carton on a sidewalk while hatted men made impious remarks to her. Headless monsters winked at her from eyes embedded in pudgy shoulders .... She suffered fainting spells, headaches and nightmares .... She complained of homesickness in letters to her mother, who promptly prayed to Kali to save Tara's conscience, chastity and complexion (p. 13).

Circumstances so contrive incidentally that she falls in love with an American. Mukherjee's description of Tara's chance meeting with David betrays her faith in the inevitable :

> Within fifteen minutes of her arrival at the Greyhound bus station there (at Madison), in her anxiety to find a cab, she almost knocked down a young man. She did not know then that she eventually would marry that young man (p. 14).

Tara's husband David Cartwright is wholly Western and she is always apprehensive of this fact. She cannot communicate with him the finer nuances of her family background and of life in Calcutta. Her failure to do so is rooted in their cultural differences. In India a marriage is not simply a union of two individuals, it is a coming together of two families as well. But in Western countries like America, a marriage is simply a contract between two individuals.

David is hostile to genealogies and often mistakes her love for family for overdependence. He asks naive questions about Indian customs and traditions and she feels completely insecure in an alien atmosphere because "Madison Square was unbearable and her husband was after all a foreigner."

After a gap of seven years Tara plans a trip to India. For years she has dreamed of this return and thinks that all hesitations, all shadowy fears of the stay abroad would be erased quite magically if she returns home to Calcutta, but it never happens. The new Americanized Tara fails to bring back her old sense of perception and views India with the keenness of a foreigner. Her entire outlook has changed. Shobha Shinde refers to this expatriate weakness, "An immigrant away from home idealizes his home country and cherishes nostalgic memories of it;"[2] and so does Tara in America but when she comes to confront the changed and hostile circumstances of her home country, all her romantic dreams and ideals crumble down. She realises that she has drowned her childhood memories in the crowd of America.

On landing at Bombay airport, she is greeted warmly by her relatives but her response is very cold and dispassionate. When her relatives address her as 'Tultul,' a nick name which they always used for her, it sounds strange to her Americanized ears. Seven years ago while on her way to Vassar "she had admired the house on Marine Drive, had thought them fashionable, but now their shabbiness appalled her" (p. 18). Her reaction towards the railway station is also one of despise. She "thought the station was more like a hospital; there were so many sick and deformed men sitting listlessly on bundles and trunks" (p. 19). In the train she happens to share her compartment with a Marwari and a Nepali. She thinks that both will "ruin her journey to Calcutta" (p. 20). The tiny Marwari is very ugly, and appears insolent while the flat-nosed Nepali is also equally disgusting. Her reaction is voiced in the following extract :

> I have returned to dry holes by the sides of railway tracks, she thought, to brown fields like excavations for a thousand homes. I have returned to India (p. 21).

With coming back to India, America looks like a dream land to her. Just a few days have passed since she left America but it seems to her that she had never been out of India, her old sense of pride comes back to her. "She had not thought that seven years in another country, a husband, a new blue passport could be so easily blotted out" (p. 25). To her, her husband David "seemed far less real than the flat-faced Nepali with extrasensory perception. She watched David's healthy face disappear into the fleshy folds of the Nepali's neck and the spider's body" (p. 26). As soon as she reaches Howrah Station, she is outraged by "the squalor and confusion of Howrah station" (p. 27). At the station, though surrounded by the army of relatives and by vendors ringing bells, beggars pulling at sleeves, children coughing on tracks, Tara feels herself completely alone. Everything looks her unreal except Bengal Tiger, her father. For a moment she thinks she might go mad. Even her father "seemed to have become a symbol for the outside world. He had become a pillar supporting a balcony that had long outlived its beauty and its function" (p. 29). When she reaches home she feels momentary peace of mind :

> After seven years abroad, after extraordinary turns of destiny that had swept her from Calcutta to Poughkeepsie, and Madison, and finally to a two-room apartment within walking distance of Columbia, strange turns that had taught her to worry over a dissertation on Katherine Mansfield, the plight of women and racial minorities, Tara was grateful to call this (her father's) restful house home (p. 33).

Staying in her paternal house she records her impressions of New York :

> New York, she thought now, had been exotic. Not because it had laundromats and subways. But because there were policemen with dogs prowling the underground tunnels. Because girls like her, at least almost like her, were being knifed in elevators in their own apartment buildings. Because students were rioting about campus recruiters and far-away wars rather than the price of rice or the stiffness of final exams. Because people were agitated over pollution.... New York was certainly extraordinary, and it had driven her to despair.... (p. 34).

She recalls how she had shaken out all her silk scarves, ironed them and hung them to make her apartment more Indian on days when she thought she could possibly not survive.

While in America Tara was always under stress, she was always conscious of her foreignness. She felt herself rootless but things do not appear better in India also. Her mother compels her to accompany her to Aunt Jharna's place to visit her ailing child infected by polio. Tara tries to sympathise with Aunt Jharna but is gravely mistaken as Aunt Jharna insults her. Tara's reaction to this is one of mutually contradictory emotions. While on the one hand she cannot sympathise with the aunt's religious attempts to heal her child, on the other she thinks : "I don't hate you. I love you, and the miserable child, the crooked feet, the smoking incense holder, I love you all" (p. 38).

Tara herself wonders at the foreignness of her spirit which does not permit her to establish an emotional kinship with her old relatives and friends :

> How does the foreignness of spirit begin? ... Does it begin right in the centre of Calcutta, with forty ruddy Belgian women, fat foreheads swelling under starched white head-dresses, long black habits intensifying the hostility of the Indian sun?

or did it

> drift inward with the winter chill at Vassar, as she watched the New York snow settle over new architecture, blonde girls ...? (p. 37).

She meets her friends but even in their company antithetical feelings beset her :

> Seven years ago she had played with these friends, done her home work with Nilima, briefly fancied herself in love with Pronob, debated with Reena at the British Council.

But now

> She feared their tone, their omissions, their aristocratic oneness (p. 43).

Tara forgets the next step of the rituals while preparing for worship with her mother and at once realizes : "It was not a simple loss ... this forgetting of prescribed actions; it was a little death, a hardening of the heart, a cracking of axis and center" (p. 51). Religion plays a central role in any culture. When she forgets the rituals it upsets her because at once she realises what America has done to her. Now she has become 'foreign' to her native values also and it fills her with a sense of rootlessness. She starts questioning the validity of her own identity.

The Catelli-Continental Hotel on Chowringhee Avenue, 'the navel of the universe' becomes her favourite place and she spends much of her time in that hotel along with her friends. There were many parties in honour of Tara's return, many teas, many dinners hosted by friends. At first Tara looks forward to these parties. She rushes to Pronob's or Reena's so that she can share reminiscences with people who understand her attitudes and mistakes. "Her friends had seemed to her a peaceful island in the midst of Calcutta's commotion. She had leaned heavily on their self-confidence" (p. 55). But gradually the beliefs and the omissions of her friends begin to unsettle her. "Her friends let slip their disapproval of her, they suggested her marriage had been imprudent, that the seven years abroad had eroded all that was fine and sensitive in her Bengali nature" (p. 55). Tara feels agitated at the lack of seriousness in the group of her friends. They want to listen to stories about America, about television and automobiles, frozen foods and record players but when she mentions ghettos or student demonstrations they protest. Tara notices a lot of change in her friends during these seven years. She cannot think of Pronob being a big industrialist. How can she tolerate his fatness and his ill-tempered nature whom she had seen as a sensitive and poetic young man. Now and then her friends and relatives make her feel guilty for marrying an American. "In India she felt she was not married to a person but to a foreigner, and this foreignness was a burden" (p. 62). Though she writes to David regularly, she fails to communicate her feelings for him. Because

> It was hard to tell a foreigner that she loved him very much when she was surrounded by the Bengal Tiger's chairs, tables, flowers, and portraits (p. 63).

How can she "describe in an aerogramme the endless conversations at the Catelli-Continental, or the strange old man (Joyonto Roy Choudhury) in a blazer who tried to catch her eye in the cafe, or the hatred of Aunt Jharna or the bitterness of slogans scrawled on walls of stores and hotels" (p. 63). Tara is totally confused. She cannot share her feelings with her friends and relatives and she fails to share things with her foreign husband. For David she is a foreigner and for her Indian friends and relatives she is a sinner who has polluted herself by marrying a 'mleccha' (outcaste). M. Sivaram Krishna blames her American husband and western education for her feelings of rootlessness and lack of identity :

> Tara in *The Tiger's Daughter* finds it difficult to relate herself to her family, city, culture in general since her marriage to an American, her western education are enough signs to brand her as an 'alienated' westernized woman. The implicit logic is that since she is exposed to the West and has absorbed its values she must be necessarily alienated. Therefore, even when she tries to 'voice' her continuing attachment for and identity with India, the voice does not carry conviction for it is at variance with the usual stance — of indifference and arrogance — one generally associates with the 'westernized' (exiled) Indian.[3]

Tara realises that America has transformed her completely. "Tara's westernization has opened her eyes to the gulf between two worlds that still makes India the despair of those who govern it."[4] In India she sees disease, despair, riot, poverty, the children eating yoghurt off the sidewalk. Now she has started looking at the ugly aspects of India. Always in her mind there is an ongoing conflict between her old sense of perception and outlook on Calcutta and her changed outlook. Jasbir Jain comments :

> Tara's consciousness of the present is rooted in her life in the States and when she looks at India anew it is not through her childhood associations or her past memories but through the eyes of her foreign husband David. Her reactions are those of a tourist, of a foreigner.[5]

Tara visits a funeral pyre at the river bank with Joyonto Roy

Chowdhury, the owner of tea estates in Assam and runs at the sight of the 'tantric' who stretches his hands for her palms. She fails to read his intentions and thinks that the man needs 'bakshees.' Is it a simple misunderstanding of tantric's intentions or Tara's inherent fear and uncertainty of her life? It seems she does not want to show her palms to the tantric because she is conscious of her sin of marrying an American without matching her horoscopes. Again her visit with Joyonto Roy to his Tollygunge compound turns out to be painful. When Joyonto Roy proposes to show her the place and says that it's a 'bustee'. Tara is all ecstatic like Western tourists :

> Is it a 'bustee'? asked Tara. She recalled frustrating moments at Vassar, when idealistic dormitory neighbours had asked her to describe the slums of India (p. 113).

The circuitous and uneven road to Tollygunge troubles her a lot. She cannot bear the dust and foul smell of squalor :

> Had Tara visualized at the start of the journey this exposure to ugliness and danger, to viruses that stalked the street, to dogs and cows scrapping in garbage dumps, she would have refused Joyonto's invitation (p. 115).

Joyonto shows her his vast compound which is now occupied by refugees and quite sentimentally tells her how he proposed his garden, etc. But Tara is hardly interested in these details :

> Tara was bewildered by her first view of the large and dusty compound. She thought if she had been David she would have taken out notebook and pen and entered important little observations. All she saw was the obvious. Goats and cows grazing in the dust, dogs chasing the friskier children, men sleeping on string beds under a banyan tree. Children playing with mud beside a cracked tubewell. Rows of hovels and huts (p. 116).

Tara loses her balance of mind when she sees a little girl suffering from leprosy. She screams and becomes almost hysteric : "Don't touch me, don't touch me!" Actually "Tara has never been a part of the crowd. She has always been sheltered, as child, young adult, and woman. Each excursion traumatizes her by bringing her closer to the touch of the masses."[6] In fact, disease, suffering, and poverty are part of existence and a common Indian ignores it or rather accepts it as an integral part of life. Tara herself once ignored all these things but her stay in States has opened her eyes to the gulf between the lives of the poor and those of the rich in her own country. Like the people of the West now she has started looking at India as a land of poor people living in a hostile, unhygienic conditions and suffering from starvation, decay and disease. Reena's mother entrusts her with the duty of mediating between them and the Irish-American Washington McDowell but her failure in understanding McDowell testifies to the fact that she has not been able to gratify the complications of American culture. America is a land of diverse cultures and people from all parts of the world have settled there. Though Tara marries an American she remains unexposed to the 'other' cultures within America. McDowell, being a black, belongs to the class of 'have-nots' in America so it is quite natural for him to join hands with the agitating crowd of labourers of Calcutta.

During the summer Darjeeling is the favourite holidaying place for the upper class families of Bengal. Along with the families of her friends Tara's family also moves to Darjeeling for a holiday trip. Darjeeling is as beautiful as ever. Tara tries to enjoy the beauties of blue mountains and natural surroundings. But her trip is marred by ugly and violent incidents. One afternoon she accompanies Pronob and an American lady Antonia on horseback around the Observatory Hill but on the way she is stopped and teased by some young hooligans. This incident leaves Tara troubled and ill-humoured. Not only this but she is also insulted by one of the members while she suggests something about the beauty contest organized by the hotel manager. The heart specialist who is one of the judges sarcastically remarks, "I think your years abroad have robbed you of feminine propriety" (p. 187). But it doesn't mean that in Darjeeling everything happens negative. Once at the special request of her religious mother, she visits Mata Kananbala Devi. She forgets all the malice and hatred for the time being and feels her soul uplifted by the 'darshan' of Mata. It is a typically Indian experience to undergo a sort of trance in a temple :

> Tara found herself shouting "Ma, Ma, Mata" with the rest. She found it easy suddenly to love everyone, even Antonia Whitehead, who was the only person standing in

> the entire room. It was not Kananbala Mata who moved her so much as the worshipers themselves (p. 173).

For the time being Tara casts aside all her suspicions and apprehensions :

> Warm and persistent tears rose in Tara's heart. She forgot her instinctive suspicions, her fears of misunderstandings and scenes, she forgot her guardedness and atrophy in that religious moment. "Ma, Ma, Mata!" She shouted with the rest (p. 173).

Here the reaction of Antonia Whitehead, who is a representative of American culture, is worthnoting :

> What India needed ... was less religious excitement and more birth-control devices. She hated confusion of issues, she said. Indians should be more discerning. They should demand economic reforms and social upheavals and throw out the Chief 'Chela' as pledge of future success (p. 175).

Tara plans a trip to Nayapur along with her whole group of friends thereafter. Nayapur is a new township in a complex of coal mines, steel foundaries and plants for hydroelectricity. It spreads across scarred little hills and forests. Tara meets the politician Tuntunwala, the same ugly Marwari fellow with whom she had shared her railway compartment while travelling from Bombay to Calcutta. Mr. Tuntunwala, the national personage, has come to plan his strategy for the elections in Nayapur. Earlier Tara has come across Mr. Tuntunwala several times. She has always felt a kind of strange attraction towards this man and so when Mr. Tuntunwala proposes to show her Nayapur she does not decline his proposal. At last this meeting ends with her claustrophobic rape by this wretched politician. Tara's failure to stop Tuntunwala from seducing her suggests that more or less she too is a party in that amorous game or she might be only a victim. It seems Tara is just ignorant of the changes that have taken place in Calcutta. Because

> in another Calcutta such a scene would not have happened. Tara would not have walked into the suite of a gentleman for medicine, and a gentleman would not have dared to make such improper suggestions to her. But except for

> Camac Street, Calcutta had changed greatly; and even Camac Street had felt the first stirrings of death. With new dreams like Nayapur Tara's Calcutta was disappearing. New dramas occurred with each new bulldozer incision in the green and romantic hills. Slow learners like Tara were merely victims (p.199).

Tara does not tell anyone of her friends about her seduction just for fear of disgrace. She realizes :

> She could not share her knowledge of Tuntunwala with any of her friends. In a land where a friendly smile, an accidental brush of the fingers, can ignite rumors — even lawsuits — how is one to speak of Mr. Tuntunwala's violence? (p.199).

The last pages of the novel are full of rapid and forceful incidents. Bharati Mukherjee brings the novel to a close on a sensational note like some Indian Hindi movie. The whole of Calcutta is burning with the violent demonstrations and riots. The labourers rising against their masters. The entire city is losing its memories in a bonfire of effigies, buses and trams :

> Tragedy, of course, was not uncommon in Calcutta. The newspapers were full of epidemics, collisions, fatal quarrels and starvation. Even murders, beheadings of landlords in front of their families.... (p. 97).

In such a situation how Tara can cope with who "longed for the Bengal of Satyajit Ray, children running through cool green spaces, aristocrats despairing in music rooms of empty palaces " (p. 105). Out of bewilderment, she plans to go back to David and calls her friends at Catelli Continental to let them know about her decision. In the meantime, the troop of marchers heads towards Catelli and she with her company gets surrounded by the mob. In an attempt to escape Joyonto Roy Chowdhury is caught in the messy crowd. Pronob tries to save him but is unfortunately killed by the mob. The novel ends with

> Tara, still locked in a car across the street from the Catelli-Continental, wondered whether she would ever get out of Calcutta, and if she did not, whether David would ever know that she loved him fiercely (p. 210).

This close of novel in the 'medias res' leaves the readers to conjecture for themselves as to what ultimately happens to Tara. Does she succeed in returning to her husband and start living happily with him keeping all her nostalgia aside or she falls a victim to the rioting mob? Once in an interview Bharati Mukherjee, said about her first novel :

> It is the wisest of my novels in the sense that I was between both worlds. I was detached enough from India so that I could look back with affection and irony, but I didn't know America enough to feel any conflict. I was like a bridge poised between two worlds.[7]

Mukherjee's statement has a force of conviction behind it in that she has also married an American, and is thus amply qualified to articulate identical responses authentically. However, her claim that she did not feel any conflict appears far-fetched. Tara Banerjee, who is identified by a majority of critics as the writer herself, finds herself sandwitched between two cultures. Her America, far from being a land of promise, is a land of violence and atrocity. It's a land of strangers and all her attempts at assimilation are destined to failure due to her 'otherness.' She breaks her family tradition and marries American David. It is also an attempt to get security in an alien land. But her marriage proves a failure because it's an emotional marriage, a decision taken impulsively. Since she has not thoroughly understood David and his socicty shc always remains nervous and apprehensive. In an attempt to Americanize herself she loses her Indian identity miserably. Tara Banerjee is not only an immigrant but she is a woman also. This makes all the difference in the Indian context. In India woman's fate is decided very early in her life because the parents start discriminating between their male and female child from the very beginning. It is incessantly hammered on the girl's consciousness that she has to move somewhere else and must be submissive and assimilative, come what may. Thus she starts a life of duality and conflict since her childhood. After marriage she undergoes a traumatic dilemma enjoined upon her to belong to an entirely new set-up. This in itself is a kind of migration — a migration from one's own former self to an imposed one. And this conflict gets multiplied with migration to another country. Tara's situation should be looked at from this angle and Brinda Bose thinks along such lines :

> Duality and conflict are not merely a feature of immigrant life in America; Mukherjee's women are brought up in a culture that presents them with such ambiguities from childhood. The breaking of identities and the discarding of languages actually begin early, their lives being shaped by the confluence of rich cultural and religious traditions, on the one hand, and the "new learning" imposed by British colonialism in India, on the other. These different influences involve them in tortured processes of self-recognition and self-assimilation right from the start; the confusion is doubled upon coming to America.[8]

Roshni Rustomji-Kerns, however, ascribes her failure to her constant nervousness regarding her role as a Bengali wife of an American :

> Tara's petulance and constant nervousness regarding her role as the Bengali wife of an American, visiting her family in Calcutta; overshadows her well-intentioned efforts to understand her world of diverse cultures.[9]

In fact, Tara's confusion results from her own "unstable self." After marrying an American she should have held fast to her decision of which she is incapable. Instead of wrestling with her predicament, she visits her native place armed with a changed perspective. Tara does not understand that "like the Bharati Mukherjee (the Authoress) of *Days And Nights in Calcutta*, (she) is an out-sider in India because of her decision to leave India, to live in North America, to marry an American mleccha (outcaste) husband.... Her sense of alienation in Calcutta is symbolised by her regular visits to Catelli-Continental Hotel, from where she views the turmoil of Calcutta from the safe heights of a tourist, cut-off from the 'real' India which seeths below her."[10]

In *The Tiger's Daughter*, Mukherjee sets about exposing how it feels for a fifteen-year-old girl to leave a sheltered home hedged by class privilege and wealth, come back to it grown to young womanhood — to come home after breaking all the social taboos by marrying a foreigner — and see whether she can find her place at home again. All the questions that impelled for answers at Vassar, she thinks, would be answered as she continues to witness the crowd's use of its numbers to surround or gherao, paralyzing movement, political demonstration, street and bustee (squatter) life, at first from the security of the balcony of the fashionable Catelli Continental Hotel and finally marooned in a car in the middle of an angry mob. But to no avail because cultural dichotomy has snapped all ties of communication. Bracketing her with the artist, Maya Manju Sharma perceptively comments :

> When Tara/Bharati goes west, she undergoes a new birth in the womb of Vassar and growth in graduate school. The new-birthed consciousness — birthed in dormitories and classrooms by a Western curriculum and consciousness — seeks to hold its history at its center where the knowledge is visionless. Like Henry James' heroine, Isabel Archer, who goes to Europe/Britain, the source of her tradition, for vision in knowledge, so Tara/ Bharati must come to the source — the omphalos of all vision — the Catelli-Continental. Thanks to Joyonto Roy Chowdhury, and her years away, Tara begins to exchange vision for insight. At the end of the novel, as she sits shivering in the Fiat, surrounded by a mob, wondering whether she will ever see her husband again, she sees the vision twinkling, pinching, pulling, slapping through the crowd that surrounds the hotel. Bharati Mukherjee is refusing to state what it is, invites a reader response in decoding the vision.[11]

Tara caught in the midst of the rioting mob marking the invisible presence of her husband David, leaves the reader stunned and wondering as the novel ends there. In a sense the turmoil outside is but an external manifestation of Tara's inner state of mind and by leaving her amidst that turmoil, perhaps, Mukherjee hints at the irreconciliability of such conflicts. Another significant ramification of cultural conflict appears in the novel discussed hereafter.

Bharati Mukherjee's second novel and a finalist for Governor General's Award, *Wife* (1975) takes up a more complex dimension of the theme of immigrant experience. It centres round the life of a middle class married Bengali woman who migrates from Calcutta to New York. After a ten year sojourn in Canada Mukherjee returned to her native country in 1973 and encountered an India which she had never anticipated : a world far less innocent than the one she remembered. During her visit to Calcutta, she got the material for this novel as she recalls, "quite by an accident, I heard the question that shaped my second novel — 'what do Bengali girls do between the ages of eighteen and twenty one...."[12]

Mukherjee opens her novel in a true Indian tradition of story-telling. The simple opening line — "Dimple Dasgupta had set her heart on marrying a neurosurgeon"[13] is quite telling and at once sets the scene that anticipates something unnatural. For Dimple Dasgupta, neuro-surgeon is a very strange choice. Mukherjee's choice of the name of the heroine as Dimple is a deliberate one and her intentions are quite explicit from the cover page of the novel where she quotes the OED definition of "Dimple" as — "any slight surface depression". From the very beginning we feel that Dimple is far from normal girls. Dimple has nothing to do except thinking about marriage because she thinks that marriage is a blessing in disguise. It will bring her freedom, fortune and perfect happiness :

> Marriage would bring her freedom, Cocktail parties on carpeted lawns, fund-raising dinners for noble charities. Marriage would bring her love (p. 3).

Dimple "thought of premarital life as a dress rehearsal for actual living. Years of waiting had already made her nervous, unnaturally prone to colds, coughs and headaches" (p. 3). Dimple is twenty but she bewails for wasted years. Nothing pleases her more than the imagination about marrying a fellow who provides her all creature-comforts. She is supposed to be studying for university examinations but books irritate her.

At last Mr. Dasgupta finds a suitable match for Dimple. Amit Basu, a Consultant Engineer is the match for Dimple. He has already applied for immigration to Canada and U.S. and his job application is also pending in Kenya. Dimple is all ecstatic about her marriage and does a lot of shopping becoming the occasion. She comes to Amit's residence at Dr. Sarat Banerjee Road after her marriage. Basus are good people but their house is not that spacious and attractive. From the very beginning Dimple does not feel easy there. She does not like Amit's mother and sister also. Her mother-in-law dislikes her name "Dimple" and wants to call her "Nandini" instead which simply infuriates the bride. However, Dimple thinks that all these problems are temporary and with the confirmation for immigration they will eventually come to an end. She frequently talks with her husband about the anticipated foreign trip though "Thoughts of living in Africa or North America terrified her" (p. 17).

Dimple Basu has always lived in a fantastic world, a world which is created by herself. But when she confronts the hard realities of life the feathers of her imagination are clipped. All her dreams crumble one by one and she is deeply upset. She thinks that waiting for marriage was better than getting married. She starts hating everything :

> She hated the gray cotton with red roses inside yellow circles that her mother-in-law had hung on sagging tapes against the metal bars of the windows (p. 20).

Her friend, Paramita Ray, whom everybody calls Pixie, had brought for her magazines in the days of waiting and she had seen in those magazines how "young marrieds" were always going to decorators and selecting "their" colours, especially their bed room colours. That was supposed to be the best part of getting married : being free and expressing yourself" (p.20). Dimple thinks that marriage has robbed her of all romantic yearnings so tastefully nourished.

One evening Amit takes her to Kwality's by taxi and orders chili chicken, chicken fried rice and chicken spring rolls. She feels uneasy handling the chicken pieces with fork and knife and thinks that it would have been better if Amit had taken her to Trinca's instead :

> He should have taken her to Trinca's on Park Street, where she could have listened to a Goan band play American music, to prepare her for the trip to New York or Toronto. Or to the discotheque in the Park Hotel, to teach her to dance and wriggle (p. 21).

Amit was not the man Dimple had imagined for her husband. When he is out of the house she starts creating the man of her dream :

> She borrowed a forehead from an aspirin ad, the lips, eyes and chin from a bodybuilder and shoulders ad, the stomach and legs from a trousers ad and put the ideal man (p. 23).

With the passing of time the excitement of marriage diminishes and she becomes pregnant, a stage known for vomitting tendency. However, her nauseating proneness is abnormal because she deliberately vomits and never leaves any opportunity of doing so at all hours of the day and night. She feels a strange sensation :

> The vomit fascinated her. It was hers; she was locked in the bathroom expelling brownish liquid from her body. She took pride in brownish blossoms.... (p. 30).

Pregnancy is a boon for Indian women because they are supposed to maintain the continuity of the clan. They are "shakti-incarnate". They are the very source of 'creation.' If a woman fails to reproduce a child she is condemned and becomes an object of hatred in society. But Dimple is singular in that "she thought of ways to get rid of ... whatever it was that blocked her tubes and pipes" (p. 31). Her killing of the mice which looked pregnant also suggests that she does not feel at ease with her pregnancy. She becomes almost hysteric in killing that tiny creature without any rhyme and reason :

> She pounded and pounded the baby clothes until a tiny gray creature ran out of the pile, leaving a faint trickle of blood on the linen. She chased it to the bathroom. She shut the door so it would not escape from her this time.... "I'll get you" she screamed. "There is no way out of this, my friend..." And in an outburst of hatred, her body shuddering, her wrist taut with fury, she smashed the top of a small gray head (p. 35).

This act of killing is a manifestation of violence is smouldering inside her. Her repulsion with her own pregnancy is born out of her hatred for Amit who fails to feed her fantasy world.

Dimple is about to migrate but she does "not want to carry any relics from her old life" (p. 42). She thinks that old things will remind her of frustrations and irritations. She counts her pregnancy also among the relics and ponders over the ways of getting rid of it. At last she decides to end it by skipping ropes. The description of her self-abortion is very poignant and touching :

> She had skipped rope until her legs grew numb and her stomach burned; then she had poured water from the heavy bucket over her head, shoulders, over the tight little curve of her stomach. She had poured until the last of the blood washed off her legs; then she had collapsed (p. 42).

This is something which only Dimple can do and her self-abortion raises serious questions regarding her very womanhood. After terminating her pregnancy she hardly gives any after thought to it. She never repents for the cruel deed she has committed by killing a prospective human life. She remains poised and dispassionate while it should have led her to an emotional upheaval. Rosanne Klass counts it as a serious mistake on Bharati Mukherjee's part and questions her understanding of Indian culture. In a review of *Wife*, she comments :

> For an Indian wife, childlessness is a disaster, pregnancy the achievement that seals her status. To overturn such ingrained values would involve a major emotional upheaval; yet Dimple acts on the vaguest and most undefined impulses, and thinks no more about it.[14]

Of course, Dimple's reactions have not been given due attention but it should be remembered that Dimple is simply an individual and her strange actions should not be equated with the values of Indian culture. In the very beginning Mukherjee has hinted at Dimple's ill mental state. In the view of some critics Dimple's act of abortion "is a sacrament of liberation from the traditional roles and constraints of womanhood."[15] Symbolically, by revoking her motherhood Dimple liberates herself from the traditional role of a Hindu wife of just bearing and rearing a child. Like the Western feminists she asserts her will but her abortive act is a kind of "moral and cultural suicide."

When Amit's confirmation for migration to U.S. comes Dimple's happiness is inexpressible. She prepares well and sees to it that nothing she misses which is necessary for a new life. She feels like being freed from the brazen fetters of servile domesticity. On the eve of their departure, Pixie organises a grand party at which she invites mostly the media persons. Dimple meets Ratna Das, a middle aged modern wife of a media brat there who does not give any importance to America. She says "It might be fun to go for a vacation... But I would not want to settle there" (p. 46). Pixie echoes the same sentiment "I wouldn't want to feel foreigner all my life" (p. 46). But this hardly deters Dimple from her resolution. For her "real happiness was just in the movies or in the West" (p. 47).

The long awaited day of migration comes and Mr. & Mrs. Amit Basu set their feet at the Kennedy Airport where Jyoti Sen, Amit's former classmate at the I.I.T., Kharagpur receives them. In the way he talks about the triple-murder case which is the talk of the town. A guy murders three persons including the ice-cream vendor just for the simple reason that the fellow doesn't have a chocolate ice-cream cone. On the way to the Sens Amit is unmindful of the scenes outside the car and is busy enquiring about job opportunities in America. Dimple feels excited and a little scared as well. She has never been to a city bigger than Calcutta and the magnificence of the city of New York terrifies her :

> She had never seen such bigness before; the bigness was thrilling and a little scray as well. She could not imagine the kind of people who had conceived it and who controlled it (p. 52).

The Sen apartment at Queens is all Indian inside. Dimple's searching eyes notice a framed batik wall hanging which shows "King Ram and his court in splendid array" (p. 53). Sens are very conscious of their identity and they never try to come out of the ghetto, their "little-India" which is around them :

> Because there are no chairs, we realise that the Sens never entertain Westerners in their home, a point confirmed in conversation noting their disgust with beef eaters and American insincerity, insecurity with the English language, and projected losses on inexpensive furniture for those returning home.[16]

The Sens' disgust with Americans and English language is quite in keeping with the feeling of insecurity in an expatriate. People raised in an entirely different social milieu and cultural atmosphere can hardly shed off their cherished values for one they are forced to adopt out of necessity. After all the thousands of professionals, doctors, engineers, management personnel etc., who migrate to America or other European countries, mostly they do it for the sole purpose of earning a high salary and after a considerable period of time to return to their native land and enjoy a life of prestige and comfort. For them the country of adoption is a temporary abode and they just try to pass their time preserving their own identity and upholding their own cultural and religious values. This is confirmed by the simple confession of Jyoti Sen :

> If it weren't for the money, I'd go back tomorrow. This is too much the rat race for a man like me (p. 55).

Getting a job in America is not an easy cake especially if you happen to be an Indian. Should one get an opportunity, it is very difficult to sustain it. There you have to bear all sorts of humiliation and exploitation without giving any vent to it. Jyoti Sen teaches Amit all tricks of the trade, the codes of conduct for an Indian professional in America to thrive :

> Work twice as hard, keep your mouth shut and you'll be a millionaire in fifteen years (p. 56).

One day Dimple goes to the market with Meena Sen and wishes to buy a cheese cake. She is afraid to go to the shop alone but when Meena encourages her she goes there. She is taut with fear and notices one by one inside the glass cake pickles, salads, hanging salamis, pink roast beef, roast duck and turkey etc. At last she reaches the shop and asks for cheese cake and the shopkeeper starts staring at her to her great embarrassment. Everywhere there is stench of blood and it is getting intolerable for her nostrils to bear the stink of beef. Instantly she fails to understand the shopkeeper and repeats her sentence. He asks whether she does not know the law and starts searching for something in his drawer. Dimple is so afraid, she thinks that the man is taking out his gun and she is left with no option but to be killed without crying. Here she realises the difference between Calcutta and New York :

> In Calcutta she'd buy from Muslims, Biharis, Christians,

> Nepalis. She was used to marry races; she'd never been a communalist (p. 60).

This very first exposure to America leaves a traumatic effect on her mind. She fails to understand the reason why a man selling beef etc. cannot sell cheese cake. What is the law of America? Did she really insult that man by asking for cheesecake? Does this provide him with sufficient reason for killing her? She runs from there for life and forgets to buy anything herself. Her bewilderment with America is due to her sheltered childhood. She had hardly ever been out of Calcutta. She did not know what might offend anybody there to cost her the precious life itself. How a boorish, an innocent Indian wife can keep her nerves in a country where murder was like flapping the bugs? Dimple thought :

> She was caught in the crossfire of an American communalism. She could not understand. She felt she'd come very close to getting killed on her third morning in America (p. 60).

The party at Vinod Khanna's place was splendid and Dimple saw Indian-Americans in flying colours. This was for the first time, Dimple happens to see so many Indians since she had left Calcutta. She realized, a "little India" had come alive. People like the Sens, Mehras, Khannas and Bhattacharyas, Miss Chakravorty all talking in familiar language. Everybody full of praise for Indian things — culture, food, habit etc. Everyone showing disgust with Americans. For them Americans are 'dirty people' who bathe only once a week. Not only this they 'use a lot of perfume'. This is just beyond Mrs. Bhattacharya's understanding why they wash their clothes in the bathroom sink in which they spit and wash their dishes? Way back to Queens Jyoti is full of praise for the feeling of unity among Indians abroad. Jyoti said :

> Wasn't it wonderful that Indians abroad were so outgoing and open minded. They didn't give a damn about communalism and petty feelings. They personally counted a number of Punjabis and Gujaratis and South Indians among their friends (p. 67).

Amit's frustration is now obvious because he finds himself still jobless. In the parties his opinion does not matter. As the days pass by, he becomes more impatient and his confidence starts shaking. This embitters his relationship with Dimple and petty-fogging becomes the order of the day. On the other hand Dimple helps Meena Sen in domestic works and spends her time in watching T.V. or reading newspapers. Dimple always lives under fear — everything terrifies her. All she hears about is murder, smugglings in the basement of the building etc. She is afraid of the policemen :

> She was scared of the policemen; they just did not look inoffensive, like the ones back home (p. 74).

The party at Mullicks (Ina and Bijoy) gives Dimple an opportunity to meet people both Indians and native Americans and study their behaviour. Here she meets Ina, the notorious wife of Bijoy Mullick for the first time. Sens and others are disgusted with this Indian lady because "she wears pants and muscara" (p. 61) and is "more American than the Americans" (p. 68). She is a chain smoker, drinks, flirts and goes to night schools. She has a particular theory about Indian immigrants :

> It takes them a year to get India out of their system. In the second year they've bought all the things they've hungered for. So then they go back, or they stay here and vegetate or else they've got to live here like anyone else (p. 76).

Indian society is a patriarchal society and it hardly permits a woman to talk of liberation and equality. Here male members decide the fate of their female counterpart. Time and again the Sens have cautioned Amit to keep Dimple out of touch with Ina, otherwise she will get corrupted by the latter's crazy ideas. It is this caution which prompts Amit to restrain her from accepting Ina's drink : "She does not like alchoholic beverages," Amit said, "she does not even like coke" (p. 77). It really astonishes the Western feminists who expect a straight answer from Dimple. It is at this party that Dimple and Amit meet Marsha Mookerji and Prodosh Mookerji — their future benefactors. For Dimple Milt Glasser, brother of Marsha is like a riddle. She is instantly attracted towards his tall and lanky personality and his courteous manners though "Dimple could not follow the way he talked, the things he talked about and the amazing leaps between his conversations" (p. 83). Later in the novel, we see how Milt plays a pivotal role.

With the passage of time, Dimple starts breaking after the realisation that she is deceived in marriage and a good-for-nothing husband like Amit will not cater for her dream world. She cannot tolerate his snores any more and insomnia becomes her accustomed habit. She suddenly realizes that "she hated the Sens' apartment, sofa-bed, the wall to wall rug" (p. 88). Now she gets disturbed at those habits of Amit which she ignored at Calcutta :

> In Calcutta she had trained herself not to see his hand (always the left) as it stopped carefully at each button, then slid up and down a few times before hanging limply at his side. But in New York these little gestures had begun to irritate her (p. 88).

Amit's unemployment was the root cause of all troubles. He was not the man Dimple had wanted as husband :

> She wanted Amit to be infallible, intractable, godlike, but with boyish charm; wantcd him to find a job so that after a decent number of years he could take his savings and retire with her to a three-storey house in Ballygunge Park (p. 89).

She thinks that her marriage to Amit is a failure of her dreams :

> She was bitter that marriage had betrayed her, had not provided all the glittery things she had imagined, had not brought her cocktails under canopied skies and three A.M. drives to dinzy restaurants where they sold divine Kababs rolled in roti (p. 102).

Her confusion with the names of the places like Nebraska and Nevada, Ohio and Iowa is only an external manifestation of the confusion growing within her mind. She is equally unhappy with her physique also because she sees herself now with the eyes of Ina Mullick. America underscores Dimple's inferiority and she contemplates ways of bringing an end to this tortuous existence. The second movement of the novel ends with Amit getting a job and with their decision to move to Greenwich in Marsha's flat.

The third and final movement is the climax marked by intense dramatic scenes punctuated with Dimple's growing abnormality. She had always dreamt of a splendid apartment fully furnished and accomplished with all sorts of appliances. Marsha's flat is like a dream come true for her. However, the burden of responsibilities in terms of watering the plants and cleaning the kitchen, etc. is to her greatly annoying. Amit feels lonely and wishes if they could have shifted near the Sens. Quite often Dimple feels irritated even over trifles. One day while Amit is reading something she complains of exhaustion which he attributes to her meagre diet. She loses her temper at this inference :

> I feel sort of dead inside and you can do is read the paper and talk to me about food. You never listen; you've never listened to me. You hate me. Don't deny it; I know you do. You hate me because I'm not fat and fair (p. 110).

The furious outburst of Dimple shows her accumulated frustrations. She is suffering from inferiority complex and thinks that she is not able to win her husband's love and affection. Amit may also be blamed for his ignorance of female psychology. He thinks that providing creature comforts is enough and hardly bothers for her emotional needs. He takes her out of four-walls very rarely and goes on admonishing instead :

> You must go out, make friends, do something constructive, not stay at home and think about Calcutta (p. 111).

To be fair to Dimple it can be said that with her deficiencies in English she could have hardly conducted herself well in a city of enormous size like New York on her own.

America has outwitted her and now she is gripped by a sense of nostalgia. It is just beyond her understanding "how could she live in a country ... where every other woman was a stranger, where she felt different, ignorant, exposed to ridicule in the elevator?" (p. 112). Her whole world is limited to the four-walls of the apartment and media becomes her only friend. She feels like writing to Pixie but drops the idea because she thinks :

> Friendship was impossible through letters. Conveying New York, Ina Mullick, her nightmares, the "phase" (as

> Amit called it) she was going through — all impossible to talk about... (p. 120).

In leisurely hours she tries to dream about Amit but fails to do so because

> Amit did not feed her fantasy life; he was merely the provider of small material comforts. In bitter moments she ranked husband, blender, color TV, cassette, tape recorder, stereo, in their order of convenience (p. 113).

Dimple's bracketing of her husband with the electronic appliances evidences that Amit is just a robot and not an actual human being for her.

Dimple's disgust with American English and American system gets accentuated even by small things. She is afraid to operate the self-service elevators. Linda Sandler explains it in terms of her traditional upbringing :

> Dimple emigrates to the electronic age with her traditional values almost intact, only partly modified by the pop culture of modern Calcutta, she is unable to make the transition from Before to After and chooses violence as a "problem-solving" device .... [17]

Dimple finds life impossible "with the people who didn't understand about Durga Pujah" (p. 114). For Indians religion is an integral part of life and Dimple's failure at assimilation with America is due to a lack of 'shared-faith.' An expatriate is tenaciously conscious of preserving his identity even in most trying moments of life. In America, she realises how easy it was to live, to communicate, to share with people in Calcutta. She never felt frightened at the sight of the policemen whose faces were so friendly, but the scene has changed completely in the new environment :

> She is scared of self-service elevators, of policemen, of gadgets and appliances. She does not want to wear Western clothes as she thinks she would be mistakenly taken for a Puerto Rican. She does not want to lose her identity but feels isolated, trapped, alienated, marginalised.[18]

At Queens Dimple had a confidante in Meena Sen with whom she could share her private feelings but at Greenwich she is all alone. Here her depression manifests itself in different ways. She fails to write to Pixie, though in her imagination she begins many a time. The greatest alter ego of a girl after marriage is her husband with whom she shares her inmost heart, but Dimple cannot do that. She keeps everything secret from Amit :

> She does not tell him about these imaginary beginnings. She didn't tell him about her immoderate day time sleeping either. They were unspeakable failings. She thought of them as deformities — sinister, ugly, wicked. (p. 115)

Dimple did have expected some trouble in the American set up when she came to this city because pain was part of any new beginning. But never in her wildest dreams had she imagined 'to be strained like this beyond endurance' :

> She had expected pain when she had come to America, had told herself that pain was part of any new beginning, and in the sweet structures of that new life had allotted pain a special place. But she had not expected her mind to be strained like this, beyond endurance. She had not anticipated inertia, exhaustion, endless indecisiveness (p. 115).

Asnani pertinently ascribes Dimple's mental state to the 'dilemma of cultures' — "Dimple is entrapped in a dilemma of tensions between American culture and society and the traditional constraints surrounding an Indian wife, between a feminist desire to be assertive and independent and the Indian need to be submissive and self-effacing."[19]

At times when loneliness becomes unbearable Dimple contemplates as many as seven ways of committing suicide. It seems as if she is in love with whatever is dark, evil, sinister, gruesome — murder, suicide, mugging these are all fascinating words for her. Even her ways of getting rid of life are fanciful like a television advertisement. She cannot trust anybody but media. Even "Her own body seemed curiously alien to her, filled with hate, malice, an insane desire to hurt, yet weightless, almost airborne" (p. 117). Linda Sandler accounts for this feeling of 'emptiness' as follows :

> She is uprooted from her family and her familiar world, and projected into a social vacuum where the media becomes her surrogate community, her global village. New York intensifies her frustrations and unhooks her further from reality.... [20]

The dinner party arranged by Amit and Dimple is appreciated by everybody. People enjoy delicious food and share jokes but Dimple is lost in her own world of reverie. Next day she sleeps till 4 o'clock and wakes up only when she feels hungry. She whispers to herself :

> She would not discuss her dreams with any one. One must draw the line somewhere; one must stand on principle. After the fifth spoonful, she realised she was not hungry, was, on the contrary, feeling ill and had spilled milk and cereal flakes on her clothes (p. 128).

Her mind is always full of news about mugging and rape; she always feels that someone is breaking her window. When Amit points out her foolishness as they occupy the 14th floor, she retorts : "In America anything is possible. You can be raped and killed on any floor" (p. 129). In a state of nervousness she hurts Amit with knife when he comes from behind to embrace her. She is all apologetic and blames America for her timidity :

> This wouldn't have happened if we had stayed in Calcutta. I was never so nervous back home (p. 132).

One day Ina Mullick comes to her in an utterly disappointed mood almost grasping — "I'm bitterly unhappy." Dimple fails to understand why Ina Mullick is so unhappy despite all her apparent fulfilments. At this moment she thinks herself lucky "to be alone among Marsha's appliances, to explore the wonders of modern American living, unencumbent by philosophical questions about happiness" (p. 136). In the meanwhile Dimple's mother Mrs. Dasgupta writes about Pixie's marriage to a 53 year old actor and this news makes her very happy. She feels glad to be the friend of a to be super actress.

Ina Mullick starts bringing her American friends to her apartment for a get together. "To Dimple they all looked alike; even their clothes were similar. She felt too shy to talk to them" (p. 146). Milt and Leni Anspach often come to her with Ina. One day Leni starts quarrelling with Ina and accuses her of spoiling her love-life with Milt. Dimple tries to pacify her but she flungs her rhinoceros shaped ashtray on the ground and breaks it. Dimple decides "it was best to regard the broken ashtray as the end of an era in her own life" (p. 148). It seems as if the broken ashtray is symbolic of freedom from servile existence for Dimple.

As the novel advances to its end, we notice Dimple anxious to settle her scores with America. Her spirit rebels, she starts going out with Ina and Milt, wears Marsha's pants etc. and enjoys all the prohibited freedom. She seduces Milt and keeps it a secret from Amit. When she goes out she puts on Marsha's tinted sunglasses because "The purple-tinted sunglasses are perhaps the most typical index of American culture. For Dimple, they are a disguise, borrowed from the west, just like Marsha's clothes and the apartment in which she is living."[21] This outing leaves her all the more confused. She turns neurotic and fails to differentiate between what she sees on T.V. and what she experiences herself in real life. She is now an alienated being undergoing the supposed after effects of alienation. One day while serving tea to Leni and Ina she engages herself in a reverie :

> After Leni removed her cup Dimple kept on pouring, over the rim of Leni's cup, over the tray and the floating dentures till the pregnant-bellied tea-pot was emptied and Leni and Ina were standing and shaking her, Dimple, Dimple, stop it! (p. 152).

She has numerous complaints against life :

> Life should have treated her better, should have added and subtracted in different proportions so that she was not left with a chimera. Amit was no more than that. He did not feed her reveries; he was unreal. She was furious, desperate; she felt sick. It was as if some force was impelling her towards disaster, some monster had overtaken her body, a creature with serpentine curls and heaving bosom that would erupt indiscreetly through one of Dimple's orifices, leaving her, Dimple Basu, splattered

> like bug on the living-room wall and rug. The catacylsm embarrassed her (p. 156).

Dimple's gloom deepens with every passing day. She starts realizing : "Her life was slow, full of miscalculations" (p. 178). Amit could only visualise the external changes in Dimple and he explains it as a case of "culture-shock." He even promises to take her to Calcutta. This does not prove helpful. Dimple starts contemplating the murder of her husband. The violence outside turns inside. She now fails to differentiate between what she sees on television and what she thinks. The idea of slaughtering her husband fascinates her. She thinks :

> She would kill Amit and hide his body in the freezer. The extravagance of the scheme delighted her, made her feel very American somehow, almost like a character in a TV Series (p. 195).

The problem with Amit is that "he lacked extravagance; he preserved in the immigrant virtues of caution and cunning" (p. 195). He fails to mark the emotional cracking-up of Dimple. "He never thought of such things, never thought how hard it was for her to keep quiet and smile though she was falling apart like a very old toy that had been played with, sometimes quite roughly, by children who claimed to love her" (p. 212). The trouble with Dimple is that she loses touch with reality. Guilts of seducing Milt and also of keeping everything a secret from Amit vex her. She loses her sleep and becomes a sleep-walker like Lady Macbeth and ultimately kills Amit without actually thinking about its consequences :

> She sneaked up on him and chose a spot, her favourite spot just under the hairline, where the mole was getting larger and browner, and she drew an imaginary line of kisses because she did not want him to think she was the impulsive, foolish sort who acted like a maniac just because the husband was suffering from insomnia. She touched the mole very lightly and let her fingers draw a circle around the detectable spot, then she brought her right hand up and with the knife stabbed the magical circle once, twice, seven times, each time a little harder, until the milk in the bowl of cereal was a pretty pink and

> the flakes were mushy and would have embarrassed any advertiser, and then she saw the head fall off — but of course it was her imagination because she was not sure any more what she had seen on TV and what she had seen in the private screen of three A.M. — and it stayed upright on the counter-top, still with its eyes averted from her face, and she said very loudly to the knife that was redder now than it had ever been when she had chopped chicken and mutton with it in the same kitchen and on the same counter... Women on television got away with murder (pp. 212-213).

The above description shows that it is a case of "cold-murder." By stabbing seven times, it seems, Dimple frees herself from the marriage tie. This is the only act of assertion she can make. Some critics are of the view that Dimple's gruesome act has nothing to do with "cultural-shock." She is not a victim of 'expatriation' but is, instead, 'a victim of her own neurotic sensibility fed on popular advertisement fantasies'. K.S. Narayan Rao looks at it from a specific angle :

> The novel raises an important question : was the Indian wife happier in India with her limited freedom and greater docility, or does she achieve happiness in her painful search for more individual freedom and in the process of maturing?[22]

No doubt, this is a valid question and one can easily clutch the matter by saying that yes, the Indian wife was not happy in Calcutta either. But if she could have stayed back she should have reconciled to her frustration. She should have been made to realise that for an Indian wife her husband is all — he is her breath and spirit and whatsoever may be his physical feature or achievement he should be loved and respected, or utmost she should have ended her own life. But the violence that is passively lying in her spirit gets multiplied on coming to America where "talking about murder is like talking about the weather" (p. 161). It is American notion of freedom for women which makes her question her own happiness and freedom. Her emotions which need outlet burst at last and she suffers feats of madness, nightmares, reveries and insomnia and what one can expect from such a heroine. Her 'splintered-self' finds solution to her problems only in murdering her husband. Thus, it is America which intensifies her confusion and turns the violence inside out and she ends up as a murderess.

The foregoing discussion demonstrates that in her first phase of creativity *i.e.*, the phase of Expatriation, Bharati Mukherjee concentrates on the individual eccentricities of her woman protagonists. While Tara Banerjee is more of an Indian girl, Dimple's character betrays an impatient and reckless trait. The end of *A Tiger's Daughter* leaves the reader guessing as to what might happen to Tara's fate, but in *Wife*, Dimple's mental abnormality leads her to kill her husband. We sympathise with and feel for Tara but Dimple's actions right from her self-abortion to the murder of Amit fail to arouse our sympathy. Other delicate aspects of immigrant tension have been explored in the two story collections which shall be taken up in the next chapter.

REFERENCES

1. Bharati Mukherjee. *The Tiger's Daughter* (Boston : Houghton Miffin, 1972; rptd. London : Chatto and Windus, 1973), p. 5. All citations followed refer to this edition.
2. Shobha Shinde. "Cross-Cultural Crisis in Bharati Mukherjee's *Jasmine* and *The Tiger's Daughter*," in R.K. Dhawan & L.S.R. Krishnasastry, ed. *Commonwealth Writing : A Study in Expatriate Experience* (New Delhi : Prestige, 1994), p. 58.
3. M. Sivaramkrishna. "Bharati Mukherjee" in M.S. Prasad, ed. *Indian English Novelists* (New Delhi : Sterling, 1982), p. 74.
4. "Oh Calcutta." *Times Literary Supplement*, 29, June 1973, 736.
5. Jasbir Jain. "Foreignness of Spirit : The World of Bharati Mukherjee's Novels," *Journal of Indian Writing in English*, 13, 2(1985), 13.
6. Maya Manju Sharma. "The Inner World of Bharati Mukherjee : From Expatriate to Immigrant," in Emmanuel S. Nelson, ed. *Bharati Mukherjee : Critical Perspectives*, *op. cit.*, p. 12.
7. Sybil Steinberg. "Bharati Mukherjee," *Publishers Weekly*, 25, August 1989, pp. 46-47.
8. Brinda Bose. "A Question of Identity : Where Gender, Race and America Meet in Bharati Mukherjee" in Emmanuel, S. Nelson, ed. *Bharati Mukherjee : Critical Perspectives*, *op. cit.*, p. 50.
9. Roshni Rustomji-Kerns. "Expatriates, Immigrants and Literature : Three South Asian Women Writers," *Massachusetts Review*, Winter 1988-89, p. 657.

10. Ralph J. Crane. "Mukherjee, Bharati" in Lesley Henderson, ed. *Contemporary Novelists* (Chicago & London : St. James Press, 1991), p. 670.
11. Maya Manju Sharma. "The Innerworld of Bharati Mukherjee : From Expatriate to Immigrant" in Emmanuel S. Nelson, ed. *Bharati Mukherjee : Critical Perspectives, op. cit.*, p. 13.
12. Quoted in Ann Mandel, "Bharati Mukherjee" in W. H. New, ed. *DLB : Canadian Writers Since 1960*, Vol. 60 (Detroit : Gale Research Company,1986), p. 267.
13. Bharati Mukherjee, *Wife* (Boston : Houghton Miffin, 1975; Penguin Indian reprint), p. 3.
14. Rosanne Klass. "Indian Wife Lives Soap-Opera Life," *MS*, October 1975, p. 88.
15. Maya Manju Sharma. "The Inner World of Bharati Mukherjee : From Expatriate to Immigrant." In Emmanuel S. Nelson, ed. *Bharati Mukherjee : Critical Perspectives, op. cit.*, p. 15.
16. Janet M. Powers. "Sociopolitical Critique as Indices and Narrative Codes in Bharati Mukherjee's *Wife* and *Jasmine*," in Emmanuel S. Nelson, ed. *Bharati Mukherjee : Critical Perspectives, op. cit.*, p. 93.
17. Linda Sandler. "Violence as a Device for Problem Solving" in *Saturday Night*, 90, 5 (October 1975), 75.
18. Enakshi Choudhury. "Images of Woman in Bharati Mukherjee's Novels" in T.S. Anand, ed. *Literary Voice*, Oct. 1995, 84.
19. Shyam M. Asnani *et al.* "Identity Crisis in *The Nowhere Man* and *Wife*," *Language Forum*, 1-2 (Jan-Dec. 1992), 42.
20. Linda Sandler. "Violence as a Device for Problem Solving," *Saturday Night, op. cit.*, p. 75.
21. Janet M. Powers. "Sociopolitical Critique as Indices and Narrative Codes in Bharati Mukherjee's *Wife* and *Jasmine*," *op. cit.*, p. 98.
22. K.S. Narayan Rao. "Review of *Wife*," *Books Abroad*, Spring 1976, 475.

4

The Phase of Transition

After the publication of *Wife* in 1975, Bharati Mukherjee took fourteen years to bring out the next novel, her *magnum opus*, *Jasmine* (1989). This interval was devoted to the writing of about two dozen short stories, each dealing with some touching aspect of rootless identity. This period was very significant from the point of view of happenings in Bharati Mukherjee's personal life as well. In the very beginning of eighties she left Canada with her husband Clark Blaise owing to disspiriting racial discriminations there. She moved to New York and tried with renewed vigour to feel at home in another culturally divergent land. The Canadian experience, however, has left its own scars and scratches on her creative personality. Through the women protagonists of her short stories, quite a few of them being her own self portraits, she unravels the trauma and exacerbations which are an expatriate's *fait accompli*. These stories have been collected in two volumes, *Darkness* (1985) and *The Middleman and Other Stories* (1988) to be analysed at the moment.

In Bharati Mukherjee's first collection of stories *Darkness* (1985) we encounter a writer who is entirely different from that of the preceding works. No longer she uses a mordant and self protective irony in describing the situation of her characters. Irony, she thinks, "promised both detachment from, and superiority over, those well-bred post-colonials much like myself, adrift in the new world, wondering if they would ever belong."[1] Here she is not an expatriate looking back to her mother country with pain and nostalgia but an immigrant who shares the common grievances of those who are like her, impelled by an insistent urge to give voice to the aspirations of these new settlers. Mukherjee sees her migration to America as "a movement away from the aloofness of expatriation, to the exuberance of immigration" (p. 3). But even after spending a couple of years in America Mukherjee cannot forget the treatment she was meted out in Canada. There she was a part of that "visible minority" which was a victim of racial discrimination and was looked upon as a pariah is treated in the Indian society. Quite a few stories of *Darkness* record Mukherjee's painful experiences as a Canadian citizen :

> In Canada, I was frequently taken for a prostitute or shoplifter, frequently assumed to be a domestic, praised by astonished auditors that I didn't have a "singsong" accent (p. 2).

Darkness is a collection of twelve stories that unfold the fates of those who have suffered among other things, racial discrimination in Canada. Explaining the background of their composition, Mukherjee writes :

> Most of these stories were written in a three-month burst of energy in the spring of 1984, in Atlanta, Georgia, while I was writer-in-residence at Emory University (p. 1).

"The World According to Hsu," one of the four stories that were written in Canada, first appeared in *Chatelaine*. Ratna, of Indian origin and her husband Graeme Clayton, a Canadian Professor of Psychology at McGill University, Montreal, are on a holiday trip at an island off the coast of Africa. The title of the story has been derived from an article by Kenneth J. Hsu in *The Scientific American* which Graem is reading at his holiday resort. Graeme has gone there to see the Southern Cross and to persuade Ratna to move from French-dominant Montreal to English-dominant Toronto where the University has offered him a chair in Personality Development. Ratna goes "to take stock of a life that had until recently seemed to her manageably capricious" (p. 37).

Both of them go there to enjoy the old fashioned vacation on the shores of the vast new ocean. They have planned to pick shells feed lemurs on the balcony of a hotel managed by a paunchy Indian, visit a colonial museum or two. However, they face another kind of adventure there, totally unwarranted and uncalled for. The beautiful island is entrapped by agitatators. There are violent demonstrations and Mr. and Mrs. Clayton are forced to remain confined to their hotel room. Clayton's casual reference to have accepted the Toronto assignment unnerves Ratna as she is terrified at the thought of living in that environment of racial hatred. She thinks :

> In Toronto, she was not Canadian, not even Indian. She was something called, after the imported idiom of London, a Paki. And for Pakis, Toronto was hell (p. 41).

Ratna's position is a peculiar one, a lost soul like other expatriates, always fighting for her real identity. The truth is that, even at this unknown obscure island she knows she cannot escape the consequences of being half — the dominant half — Indian owing to her mixed origin.

While the Clayton couple is caught in the curfew of the island and is forced to remain within the confines of Hotel Papillon, Ratna is not afraid of the violence outside. She is, rather, happy that the curfew outside delays her departure to Toronto. She recalls the harrowing tales of Pakis' being discriminated against in Toronto. Graem Clayton is hardly aware of her emotional upheaval. She cannot forget how

> A week before their flight, a Bengali woman was beaten and nearly blinded on the street. And week before that an eight-year-old Punjabi boy was struck by a car announcing on its bumper : KEEP CANADA GREEN. PAINT A PAKI (p. 47).

Graem tries to cheer her up saying "It won't happen to you." And again, "Look — violence is everywhere. Toronto's the safest city on the continent" (p. 47). At this she promptly retorts : "Sure," she said, "for you" (p. 47).

Nothing can alley her fears and another event flashes in her mind. She recalls how "An Indian Professor's wife was jumped at a red light, right in her car. They threw her groceries on the street. They said Pakis shouldn't drive big cars" (p. 47). Ratna's fears correspond to the experiences of the author herself which finally resulted in her departure from Canada. For Ratna her foreignness is better than going to Toronto. Here at this island at least, she is not the "other," a dark-skinned Euracian. She can enjoy her dinner and have her time with other tourists without any apprehension.

At the end of the story motley tourists, confined to the seedy hotel room due to curfew, dine while sharing with one another their reactions to the happenings outside. In the meantime, when her husband defies the curfew and stumbles out to search for the Southern Cross,

> She saw that the label on the bottle read : 'Cote de Cassandre.' A superior red table wine that no one had ever heard of : perhaps the lone competent industry on the island... She poured herself another glass, feeling for the moment at home in that collection of Indians and Europeans babbling in English and remembered dialects. No matter where she lived, she would never feel so at home again (pp. 55-56).

While the critic Christine Gomez considers that the world view of Hsu here becomes a "metaphor," he also thinks that "Hsu's one-world weltansschuung" becomes an "unattainable ideal." His idea is that "There is perhaps a longing for the world according to Hsu, a one world free from cultural collisions, dilemmas and separation."[2] But unfortunately that proves a mere hollow dream. Here we have a world that is based on sharp racial distinctions. There is a feeling of "otherness" for those "Pakis" who have come to Canada covering almost half of the world.

The end of the story raises problematic questions regarding the vision and judgement of the novelist. C. L. Chua comments :

> If being "at home" means feeling at ease, secure and free from conflict, then she is deluding herself. The inescapable fact remains that Ratna is shunned as a 'white rat' in India (p. 44) and scorned as a 'Paki' in Canada; furthermore, she is clearly an alien on that island, surrounded by tourists (derogatorily described as "that collection") who are without homes there, 'babbling' at each other without a common unifying language, in a country without political stability. Therefore, although the final sentence of the story appears to be too easily

> optimistic ... it could alternatively be read as an ironic and despairing assessment by Mukherjee that Ratna will never really be 'at home' anywhere.[3]

This story deserves to be called a fine expatriate study with all the apprehensions and duality that shroud an individual in an alien atmosphere.

The other story "Isolated Incidents" marks a departure in that the expatriate experience is viewed from the point of view of a native Canadian, Ann Vane, whose job is to file complaints from immigrants against problems concerning Human Rights. Two specific cases of racial discrimination in Toronto are brought to her notice — that of Dr. (Miss) Supariwala and John Mohan Persawd.

Doctor (Miss) Supariwala is "a stern, stocky woman of fortythree, with doctorates from Western Ontario and Bombay" who claims "to have been passed over at job interviews in favour of lesser candidates. She is a Canadian citizen, has published numerous articles and honoured with a few research grants as well. Her promptness, discipline and preparedness is beyond question, but she is denied the job on flimsy grounds. The interviewers think "students would not relate easily to her, some might complain of her accent, her methodological stiffness, her lack of humor" (p. 79). Miss Supariwala thinks that she is a victim of racial discrimination and probably rightly so. She represents her claim like other Canadians, which irritates Ann who thinks it strange that even after facing so much of problems these expatriates still find reasons for staying on in Canada.

The other case is that of Persawd, John Mohan and relates to a subway assault — "Queen Street Station this time : chipped teeth, cut lips, broken nose, blackened eyes. Cuts, abrasions" (p. 82). His frustration explodes in these words :

> "Canadians are mean as hell," says John Mohan Persawd. "Life is hopeless man, no justice, no redress."

To this Ann replies :

> I don't know about that... If this had happened in New York you'd have been left for dead.

Persawd's relative lawyer interrupts :

> Correction, Miss Vane... If this had happened in New York, he'd have been mugged for his money, not racially assaulted (p. 84).

Violence in America, Mukherjee implies, is ubiquitous and terrible, but at least it has no tinge of partiality on ethnic grounds. Ann's defensive posture does not mean that she is at all blind to these atrocities. In the beginning "she had tried too earnestly to correct the nation's wrongs. Now she saw problems only as a bureaucrat. Deal only with the sure things. Pass the others off. Get documentation. Promise nothing" (p. 81). Ann Vane's detached view caused partly by her job-constraints, is tinged with irony. She knows the futility of her work in documenting such cases. Nothing would ultimately come out of it at all :

> Torontonians were proud of their subway, their politeness, proud of their moral spotlessness. This, after all, was not New York. Assault on John Mohan Persawd and dozens like him would always be considered isolated incidents and not racial (pp. 82-83).

Thus Mukherjee stresses in this story that in Canada the fate of immigrants is sealed and they can never 'feel at home' there. They are destined to suffer and live a hellish life and cases of discrimination or hostility towards the visible minority will not be related to racism but will always be ignored as "Isolated Incidents," not worthy of serious import.

In "Hindus," written in Canada, but set in the U.S.A., Mukherjee juxtaposes an expatriate against an immigrant to draw out the contrast. Leela Lahiri, the narrator of the first person narrative reveals an immigrant's fluid identity. She proudly declares, "I am an American Citizen" (p. 133) but she is also proud of her Bengali Brahmin past. H.R.H. Maharajah Patwant Singh of Gotlah is an obvious expatriate who nurses his grievances against India. When Maharajah and Leela meet after two years, the Maharajah is writing his memoirs to record his pain and grievances. Leela, on the other hand celebrates rebirth in a new world but a cautious reader finds traces of Indian sensibility in her. For her, being a newborn immigrant does not mean totally denying her Hindu past. Leela frankly acknowledges her duality — her basic Hindu imagination and her immigrant American sensibility.

She cannot tolerate being called a 'niece' of Maharajah Patwant Singh because she is not blind to her 'caste-superiority' in India : 'I was a Bengali Brahmin; Maharajas ... were frankly beneath me, by at least one caste' (p. 133). She is a rebel who has married to Derek, a whiteman, and has 'broken cast etiquette' she disclaims 'any recent connection with India' but still for her 'home' is India, as she adds 'I haven't been home in ages" (p. 133). She is aware of her origin from Vishnu's knee. We see her as a well-settled immigrant who can marry a whiteman and can separate at will (as she does with Derek). A typical Indian Hindu wife can never think of separation from her husband. In two years she has "tried to treat the city (New York City) not as an island of dark immigrants but as a vast sea in which new Americans like myself (herself) could disappear and resurface at will" (p. 136). She neither complains against India nor finds Indianness as a barrier in her adjustment.

Patwant Singh's 'negative nostalgia' manifested in his character offers a foil to her thinking. He is a typical expatriate and the ghost of past haunts his ways wherever he goes. He is not at ease with the 'dhoti' wallas of his country :

> The country has changed totally ... Crude rustic types have taken over. The 'dhoti-wallas'... they would wrap themselves in loincloths if it got them more votes. No integrity, no finesse. The country's gone to dogs (p. 135).

He cannot forget those insults that were heaped upon him in his country. When he thinks about his days in India his sense of loss and deprivation surfaces to the floor :

> The country has no respect anymore. The country has nothing. It has driven us abroad with whatever assets we could salvage (p. 135).

And again,

> 'I have nothing,' he spat. 'They've stripped me of everything. At night I hear the jackals singing in the court-yard of my palace' (pp. 135-36).

He finds solace only in writing — "writing is what keeps me from going through death's gate. There are nights..." (p. 138) though he leaves it only unfinished. Patwant Singh's past is an impediment in the process of his cultural absorption. Leela's Indian convictions are too tough to be shaken :

> An Indian woman is brought up to please. No matter how passionately we link bodies with our new countries, we never escape the early days (p. 139).

This fact refers to the Indianness of Bharati Mukherjee also. She has always tried to negate her Indianness in her statements and interviews but her subtle sense of Indian values is always implicitly in the background of her writings.

Bharati Mukherjee uses language as a metaphor in this story for an imposed sense of "otherness." One of the characters Lisa comments on Leela's language as 'Hindu' — this irritates Leela and she thinks of refuting her. However she realises :

> No matter what language I speak it will come out slightly foreign, no matter how perfectly I mouth it. There is a whole world of us now, speaking Hindu (p. 140).

The above statement shows that Leela with all her attempts at assimilation remains the "other" for the native Canadians.

Except for "Courtly Vistion," the remaining stories in this collection were written after Mukherjee's migration to the U.S.A. and their protagonists are mainly immigrants. If the expatriate sensibility is probed in these stories, it is to its disadvantage. In "Angela," the protagonist is an orphan girl from Dhakka subjected to war-time atrocities in the past and now adopted by the Brandons in the U.S.A. Angela is a well settled immigrant with no nostalgic longing for her native country Bangladesh and no hatred for it either. She continually draws contrasts between Bangaldesh and America with cool detachment and total objectivity :

> I am Angela the Angel. Angela was sister Stella's name for me. The name I was born with is lost to me, the past is lost to me. I must have seen a lot of wickedness when I was six, but I can't remember any of it. The rapes, the dogs chewing on dead bodies, the soldiers. Nothing (p. 13).

One of her sisters (Daughter of her New Parents) Delia is in coma and is being attended by a Doctor from Goa, India, Vinny Menezies. Vinny loves Angela. 'Only a doctor could love this body,' she thinks, aware of her scars (pp. 19, 11). In America 'for less than two years' (p. 9), Angela has been 'forced to assimilate' (p. 17) : a high-school cheer leader, she speaks of her newly acquired Iowan 'sisters' and her 'Dad,' she knows how to soothe grief with Diet Coke (p. 9) and she has learned to enjoy a Sunday pork roast because 'pigs aren't filthy creatures here as they are back home' (p. 14).

Vinny Menezies is the most sympathetic of Mukherjee's Indian physicians; he is both innocuous and ridiculous. He is depicted through the point of view of Angela, the teenaged orphan high school student. This immigrant physician from Bombay is old-fashioned but cultured. He routinely appreciates Angela's Sunday afternoon piano playing with exclamations of "bravo" (p. 17). In the manner of the old country, Menezies seeks a bride in a marriage of convenience. He seeks to combine this search with altruism. Therefore, the object of his affections becomes the Old World Orphan Angela. As Mitali R. Pati comments :

> Mukherjee's art of characterization depends heavily upon contrasting the public and private selves of her principal character.... [4]

It is remarkable to note how Dr. Menezies is different from Menezies, the lover :

> In the hospital he seems a man of circumspect feelings, but on Sunday afternoons when we drive (as Angela discloses) around and around in his Scirocco, his manner changes. He seems raw, aimless, lost (p. 13).

Again, we see that the well settled American narrator (Angela) is different from the one who is cherishing the nightmares of 1971 war of Bangladesh. Salvaging the childhood memories, she recalls :

> Delinquents and destitutes rush me. Legless kids try to squirm out of ditches. Packs of Pariah dogs who have learned to gorge on dying infant flesh, soldiers with silvery bayonets, they keep coming at me, plunging their

> knives through my arms and shoulders. I dig my face into the muddy walls of a trough too steep to climb. Leeches, I can feel leeches gorging on the blood of my breasts (pp. 19-20).

But still she is always hopeful of her better future. She is always aware that she has been "saved for a purpose" (p. 19).

In her narrative, Angela feels no passion for Menezies, but being an orphan from the East, she realizes that her middle-aged suitor offers financial security and the secret desire of his raw and wild heart. As she contemplates accepting Menezies, she is aware of her own body mutilated in childhood by soldiers. The South Asian immigrant woman in Angela betrays no passion for Menezies, nor any desire for a more erotic relationship for herself. The cutting off of her nipples at the age of six has left her unable to feel positively about her own sexuality. Between the war atrocity which she has left behind and the powerful call of the traditional male in Menezies, Angela remains enmeshed in the net of Old World patriarchy. Her belief in her own assimilation into the American melting pot is therefore ironic.

In Mukherjee's *Darkness* many women immigrants are wives who accompany their husbands overseas and have no central say in whatever happens. Two such women are the characters in the stories "The Lady from Lucknow" and "Visitors." Nafeesa Hafeez, the narrator and heroine of the story "The Lady from Lucknow" is a daughter of an army doctor. After partisan the family of Nafeesa moves to Rawalpindi in Pakistan from Lucknow. At 17 she marries a "good man" (p. 24) Iqbal, who works for IBM and she has followed him from Pakistan to Lebanon, Brazil, Zambia, France and eventually to Atlanta, Georgia. She has two children. Iqbal feels very insecure in America and refers to himself as "not quiet" (p. 25). On one occasion while making fun of the American preoccupation with sex, "he lungs for ... (her) breasts in mock passion" (p. 24).

As far as Nafeesa is concerned, though hers was an arranged marriage at seventeen, she has always yearned for passionate pleasures defying all taboos like the girl next door in Lucknow. Thus her "first-person narrative indirectly contrasts the puritanical upbringing of Islamic women with her own craving for romantic and sexual fulfilment."[5] In America, Nafeesa tries for a life of passion by loving a 65 year old white man. Committing adultery in the absence of their husbands is a common affair among these immigrant women. These 'discretions are deliberate' and only those women are 'caught in mid-shame' who want to get out (p. 25). Nafeesa thinks herself very lucky in winning the love of a white man. James Beamish, her white lover, is an ardent flatterer. He makes Nafeesa feel "beautiful, exotic, responsive" (p. 25). Her liaison with Beamish is not only an attempt to express her independence and individuality, but it also gives her an illusion that by carrying on an illicit affair she is somehow identifying herself with America. She is mildly disillusioned, however, when after she has gone to the trouble of acquiring a front closing bra and silky new underwear for her first assignation, her lover wears "an old T-shirt and lemon-pale boxer shorts" (p. 30). This is not the drama she had anticipated. Mukherjee's South Asian Madame Bovary's romance crumbles as she is discovered in bed unexpectedly by Beamish's wife who is too used to her husband's infidelities to care. This confrontation, however, far from being explosive or dramatic turns out to be a ridiculous affair. Kate, Beamish's wife, sees her as an exotic capable of provoking only a passing interest in her husband. Here we see that Nafeesa changes nothing by her passion and has no desire to die either. One recalls that women's adultery can be severely punished by the Old Islamic law of the Lucknow lady's origins. In Atlanta, there is no anger, no violence, no vengeance as there might be in Lucknow where the beaten romantic teenage girl died of a broken heart in Nafeesa's opening flashback.

Suddenly Nafeesa sees herself caught in a different patriarchal paradigm, that of the white man's coloured mistress in a new version of the colonial era. Her realization of her own exploitation as a sexual object is ironic because she has only exchanged the polygamous code of Islamic tradition for white male patriarchy in America. Mitali R. Pati comments :

> The conflict in the social and cultural codes of the East and the West, the old and the new shows the hopelessly

> binary nature of all human desire. For the diasporic Indian, love symbolises the anarchy of the self.[6]

This explains the situation of both Nafeesa and Vinita, the heroine of the story "Visitors". Both try to break the taboos of their traditional cultures and ultimately end up in a mess.

In "Visitors", Vinita, a beautiful Indian girl, accepts an arranged marriage, and six days after wedding, she takes "an Air India flight to Citizenship in the New World" (p. 162). Her husband Sailen Kumar, "a well-mannered and amiable-looking man, a St. Stephen's graduate who had gone on to London University and Harvard and who now worked for a respectable investment house in Manhattan" (p. 162). He lives in a two-bedroom condominium with access to gym, pool and sauna across the river, is ambitious and intends to become a millionaire in New York City. He and his friends are concerned, however, about becoming "too American" (p. 165), no doubt because their nostalgic bond with India gives them a kind of security, and because they realise that their racial and cultural difference makes it impossible for them to be completely assimilated in the New World. Consequently, while the men go out to work in Manhattan, the women are expected to remain at home and create a form of India in their expensive condominiums.

Now and then Vinita refers to her experiences in this New World. She is bewildered at the fast pace of life in America :

> In America, at least in New Jersey, everyone Vinita meets seems to acknowledge a connection between merit and reward. Everyone looks busy, distraught from over work. Even the building's doorman; she worries about Castro, the doorman. Such faith in causality can only lead to betrayal (p. 163).

Vinita had expected that married life in a new country with no relatives around, should change her. She had thought "overnight she would become mature, complex, fascinating : a wife instead of a daughter" (p. 164). She notices a change but this change far from being positive is something anarchic :

> It's nothing specific. She considers fear of newness a self-indulgence, quite unworthy of someone who has wanted all along to exchange her native world for an

> alien one. The slightest possibility of disruption pleases her (p. 164).

The world of America, which she knows mainly from the soap operas she watches on television while her husband is at work, seems to offer adventure and an opportunity "to size up the situation and make up one's own rules" (p. 167). It also offers the kind of passion she does not know with her husband, and she often imagines herself "on the television screen, in the roles of afternoon wives taken in passion" (p. 171). She is content at first to experience this excitement vicariously, until she receives a visit, in her husband's absence from a young Indian student who comes wearing sneakers and a baseball cap and advises her to forget certain traditional ways of doing things in favour of "American shortcuts" (p. 169).

She realises that rules in America are different from those back home. An Indian wife would never allow any stranger in her house when her husband is away. She lets Rajiv Khanna come in and to take liberty (to some extent only) with her. She does not feel like calling her husband. She has heard Mrs. Thapar saying that very afternoon :

> We may have minted a bit of money in this country, but that doesn't mean we've let ourselves become Americans. You can see we've remained one hundred percent simple and "deshi" in our customs (p. 168).

She also wants to remain 'deshi' but her duality is clear from the way she enjoys the freedom of America. Her 'deshi' attitude will not let her loose to enjoy the company of that good looking young man. She knows that "letting him in might lead to disproportionate disaster" (p. 168) still in her heart of hearts she wishes to enjoy the licentiousness of American society.

After her visitor departs, Vinita puts on a purple silk sari, cooks for her husband and the friends he brings home without warning her a six course dinner and ecstatically "serves the men and manipulates them with her youth and beauty and her unmaskable charm. She has no idea that she is on the verge of hysteria" (p. 176). While her husband treats her like the queen of his heart, she is never really involved in his life, and his relationship with her is based on the erotic rather than the passionate love. She is his goddess, but he controls her completely, especially when she exerts erotic power over him. In India, Vinita might have had to fulfil simultaneously the roles of goddess and whore to her husband; she might never have experienced passion in her marriage because such emotions were irrelevant to her status as wife, but she would not have been tautalized, as she was in America, by the possibility of passion and self-expression. Mukherjee emphasizes Vinita's repression in America by imprisoning her in the phony schizophrenic American/Indian condominium, while allowing her visitors to come from and go out into the exterior world.

"A Father" is another fine story in the collection dealing with the problem of reconciliation between the Indian and the American values. Mitali R. Pati comments :

> The self-division experienced by Mukherjee's Indian men as they encounter the sexual liberation of the new country leads to acts of shame, madness, even violence....[7]

The above statement is aptly suitable, in the context of Mr. Bhowmick, the hero of the story. We see how a "patriarch" is brought to shame, violence, even madness in America when he contends with his bright, unmarried, engineer daughter's artificially inseminated pregnancy. Bhowmick, formerly a provincial from Ranchi, is a henpecked husband who begins by living in awe of his clever professional daughter Babli. Dominated by his wife, whose dowry was Bhowmick's education at Carnegie Tech., he emigrated to the United States because of his wife's nagging. Despite his lack of power, Bhowmick worships Kali, the goddess of wrath and vengeance. In "A Father," Mr. Bhowmick wonders how he could 'tell these bright mocking women,' his sceptical wife and daughter,

> that in the 5.43 a.m. darkness, he sensed invisible presence : gods and snakes frolicked in the master bedroom, little white sparks of cosmic static crackled up the legs of his pajamas. Something was out there in the dark, something that could invent accidents and coincidences to remind mortals that even in Detroit they were no more than mortal (p. 61).

How, indeed, can he speak of quintessential Hindu darkness when his wife shouts in idiomatic American English, "Hurry it up with the prayers" (p. 60) and his engineer daughter, Babli — graduate of Georgia Tech — tells him : "Face it, Dad... you have an affect deficit?' (p. 61) In the pre-dawn darkness he prays to the image of Kali, 'the patron goddess of his family' in Ranchi (p. 60). Babli is not tolerant of superstitions as Mr. Bhowmick hears her muttering : "This Hindu myth stuff is like a series of supergraphics" (p. 65). Thus while Mr. Bhowmick is predominantly an expatriate his wife and daughter are well adjusted immigrants. He is nostalgic about the feminine and tender women of his youth. He is disappointed that his daughter Babli, an electrical engineer, is not feminine enough for him. No doubt that Mr. Bhowmick is "a modern man, an intelligent man" (p. 64) but still he is prudent enough "to know that some abiding truth lies bunkered within each wanton Hindu superstition" (p. 64). He is always caught in the mess of his native culture but still trying hard to cope with the new one. A dozen times a day he repeats the words "compromise" and "adaptability," and always tries to find a common thread of synthesis between "new-world reasonableness and old-world beliefs" (p. 64). When he discovers his daughter's pregnancy, though traditional thoughts of family honour upset him he is happy that someone had found her feminine and lovable. His shock turns to violence when he hears that she has gone in for artificial insemination out of hatred for men :

> who needs a man? The father of my baby is a bottle and a syringe. Men louse up your lives. I just want a baby (p. 72).

He starts attacking his pregnant daughter with a rolling pin. The eruption of violence in him is due to his inability to reconcile the wistful expatriate in himself with the immigrant in his militantly feminist daughter. Thus the inadequacy of the expatriate and his inability to cope with immigrant life has been fully brought out in this story.

In the story "Nostalgia," the protagonist is Dr. Manny Patel, a psychiatric resident at a state hospital in Queens, New York. He has chosen to settle in the U.S.A. and has married a white lady, Camille. He resents being called a Paki scum even by a schizophrenic like Mr. Horowitz. Quite ironically the author comments : "He was not one nostalgia; he was not an expatriate but a patriot" (p. 98).

While all through the story we encounter a man who searches every solution to his problems in Indian things. He enjoys his American house, his car, loves his family and his acquisitiveness is entwined with love. America has been very good for him but still :

> He lived with the fear that his father would die before he could free himself from the crazies of New York and go home. He missed his parents, especially his father, but he could not explain this loss to Camille (p. 99).

He is the only child of his parents born out of the blessings of goddess Parvati in their old age. So he thinks that he should go to India to look after his parents. If not out of love for his parents at least as a sense of duty to the goddess. Now and then he reflects that "money, luxuries : he could have both in India, too" (p. 100). One day in such a mood he drives to Manhattan. Amid the chaos of New York's "Little India" on that busy afternoon he is smitten by a youthful sales girl in an Indian grocery store. Nostalgia for the subcontinental romantic fantasies of his youth grips Patel. His romantic desires have been long suppressed in his stable marriage with the nurse Camille (who had done most of the pursuing during their courtship). Seeking an escape from his expensive and highly organized life in the suburbs, Patel experiences a sharp desire to sleep with the Indian beauty Padma.

Manny Patel's adultery is the literal rendering of a series of South Asian cultural cliches. Padma is named after the tropical flower lotus. She has a curvacious body like a Bombay film star. The omniscient third-person narrator stresses that Patel is a loving husband and father dominated by acquisitiveness. In his affair with Padma, Patel combines his acquisitiveness with nostalgia for the style of life in the old country where he continues to own a home. He is divided in his desire to be within both cultures, Eastern and Western, simultaneously.

After a stereotypical spicy dinner in an expensive Indian restaurant, Patel's inevitable sexual encounter with Padma takes place. However, this encounter is destined to be a painful experience for Dr. Patel because Padma is nothing else but a prostitute. Right in the beginning a doubt creeps in the mind of Dr. Patel when

Padma agrees for a dinner with him but Dr. Patel could not resist this temptation of sleeping with an Indian empress :

> The Indian food, an Indian woman in bed, made him nostalgic .... He wished he had married an Indian woman. One that his father had selected. He wished he had any life but the one he had chosen (p. 111).

However, Dr. Patel's erotic daydream disintegrates, in the typical style of Bombay films, with the entry of the card board villain — the waiter who is a pimp of Padma. Dr. Patel is blackmailed by the waiter for raping the so-called "underage" (p. 111) Padma. After writing a cheque for $700 and promising a medical note for immigration officers, Patel defecates in the sink of the motel bathroom and writes "WHORE" (p. 113) on the mirror and floor with his own feces. Thus we see that the expatriate element of nostalgia is exposed as a weakness, a chink in Dr. Patel's immigrant armour in this story.

The next story 'Tamurlane,' which first appeared in *The Canadian Forum,* is perhaps the most graphic story about Canadian racism. It deals with the sad plight of illegal immigrants. The story derives its title from the Central Asian warrior king, decisively nicknamed Timur, the lame. It is a first person narration by a male illegal Indian who works as a waiter in a Toronto restaurant. These illegal Asian immigrants are always under stress. Neither they have hopes for a better future nor the calm of mind at present. They are constantly struggling with the fear of being caught by the Canadian police. As the narrator reveals :

> We sleep in shifts in my apartment, three illegal on guard playing carols and three bedded down on the mat on the floor. One man next door broke his leg jumping out of the window. I'd been whistling in the bathroom and he had mistaken it for our warning tune. The walls are flimsy (p. 117).

He keeps three other Indian illegal workers in his apartment, all desperately trying to evade being deported. "Nights I hear collective misery. Was this what I left Ludhiana for?" (p. 117). He regrets the environment has changed his old prejudice :

> I have been too long here; there was a time when I would tell them all apart not just Hindu and Muslim, but where, what caste and what they were hiding. Now all I care about is legal and illegal (p. 118).

'Tamurilane' is concerned with the Indian-Canadian Cook, who works as a Tandoor chef in an Indian restaurant called Mumtaz Bar B-Q in Toronto, owned by one Mr. Aziz. Gupta, the tandoor chef, though a legal immigrant works in a restaurant that mostly employs illegal immigrants. He is crippled from being pushed in front of a Toronto subway train by Canadian racists and ever since can only move rigidly with crutches. His legs had been seriously damaged. He was a pathetic figure indeed, yet not willing to leave Toronto despite all injustice and cruelty. In the restaurant Gupta is being encouraged to go to the States by an enthusiastic sponsor. The US is another location in which to hide where "those who can run do", but Gupta refuses to yield to the man's solicitations. Again the man urges "If you stay here, trouble is going to find you. Get out while you can" (p. 121). He recounts his own heroic odyssey :

> You remember the time I was running to catch that train from Grand Central and I was stopped by a cop? He thought I was a Puerto Rican, remember, and because he had never seen an Indian run before I started running, when out pop three young chaps from an arcade. One boy knocked me down. Actually he tripped me, so it looked like an accident. Then the other two spat on me, called me names, you wouldn't believe. I'm a Gandhian of the old school. All the time the hooligans were belaboring me, my friend, I was thinking of you (p. 121).

The time to run under cover came at five minutes after five and all ran to hide : "That wasn't the first time. We knew where to hide ... we could hear the mounties up in the kitchen and we didn't know how Gupta would handle himself. The mounties found them all hiding and took them up to the kitchen. "There is another one," said the immigration man. "You too," said the mounties, pointing to Gupta, "We are all going to the Station." Gupta resists : "This is a business establishment. I am responsible here while the owner is away." But it is of no avail. They say, "We are closing you down, when the owner comes back we'll get him too" (p. 124). The story centres round this raid on illegals at the restaurant The fatal encounter between Asian illegal and Canadian police and immigrant officers is most terrible yet to their taste and liking.

Gupta, the chef, refuses to submit his ground even when all others have scattered because of the raid. Leaning against a counter to support his crippled legs, he orders the intimidating mounties out of his kitchen : "Get out of my kitchen," said Gupta, "Get out immediately." They warn him not to resist but he fearlessly replies "I am not resisting. I am ordering you away from here" (p. 124). What follows is a horrifying scene of a violent struggle that is both ruthless and tragic. Whcn the mounties try to take Gupta despite his ordering them out, he grabs a cleaner and slashes the mounties outstretched arm. Then he pulls out his Canadian passport — the proof of his legitimacy — and holds it defiantly in front of his face — sitting up. "That way, he never saw the drawn gun, nor did he try to dodge the single bullet" (p. 125). Thus, this story "takes us to the world of illegal immigrants constantly under the fear of being caught and punished yet determined to live in these circumstances,"[8] observes Sudha Pandya.

The next story in the collection "The Imaginary Assassin" has a young male narrator attracted to saints, a Sikh born in Yuba city, California in 1960. While other American kids "had their rock stars to make life bearable" (p. 181), he had his mythic stories of family members. He talks to his Grandfather who claims to have killed Gandhi, although someone else was caught for the murder. The Grandfather explains why he wanted to kill Gandhi--because of the brutalization of the Sikhs, particularly of the women, and of others during partition.

The boy loves his Grandfather the first settler in the Valley to work as a farmer. But his grandfather is homesick, went back to India after a shop-lifting episode and then returned in 1948, a month after the assassination of Gandhi. He is a typical expatriate who nurses his grievances against the country of adoption :

> California was paradise to starving men from dusty Ludhiana villages. But what good was access to paradise if you weren't happy? The first time around, California

> had made Grandfather homesick. All the Sikhs in America, Grandfather'd complained, were knock-kneed and weakly. They'd lost their 'dum,' their zest, as soon as they'd landed overseas (pp. 179-80).

The narrator boy himself is not happy with his life in Yuba city :

> "The shabby diligence of our immigrant lives in Yuba city shamed the romantic in me," he claims. (p. 180)

He is much inclined to his Sikh roots and does not want to take up the ordinary life as a engineer, his parents have planned for him. Instead, he dreams of the Sikh warrior tradition of Sirhan B. Sirhan. His grandfather's stories have magic and miracles in their 'headless ghosts, eager to decapitate, could hide in trees along dark country lanes" (p. 181). The boy hears 'the cackle and swish of windblown headless ghosts.' And we are surprised that "even a nine-year-old American boy with good grades can confess his fear of gods and unholy spirits" (p. 183).

The story explains the psychology of Sikhs while letting us see the other side of the sainthood of Gandhi : the price others pay such that "Gandhi the celibate was the biggest rapist in history" (p. 187). Is the story true? Yes, as a work of the imagination. The end connects up with the "real world" : a slender, modern houseguest is picked up by the Yuba City police because they say "he'd killed another Sikh in Toronto, Canada. I don't know how, or why, or when" (p. 191). Peter Nazareth finds that the story suggests "sainthood and violence lie very close together." He observes :

> Sainthood can be the cause of and justification for violence. On the other hand, as we have seen, certain types of "violence" are committed by people we can call secular saints — people whose actions make survival and growth possible for themselves and for others.[9]

In the miniature painting described by Bharati Mukherjee in "Courtly Vision," the final story of *Darkness*, we see an emblem of Mukherjee's own art, an example of inter-textuality in which the description of a painting becomes a text that provides the entire book with a means of interpreting it and of justifying its formal and semantic peculiarities. Mukherjee's anonymous painter depicts 'Count Barthelmy, an adventurer from beyond frozen oceans'

(p. 195), admiring 'a likeness of the Begum, painted on a grain of rice by Basawan, the prized court artist' (p. 195); at the end of the story, the Emperor Akbar — third and most notable of the six great Mughal emperors — cries out :

> Give me total vision, commands the emperor. His voice hisses above the hoarse calls of the camels. You, Basawan, who can paint my Begum on a grain of rice, see what you can do with the infinite vistas the size of my opened hand. Hide nothing from me, my co-wanderer. Tell me how my new capital will fail, will turn to dust and these marbled terraces be home to jackals and infidels. Tell me who to fear and who to kill but tell it to me in a way that makes me smile. Transport me through dense fort walls and stone grilles and into the hearts of men (p. 199).

As he leads his army out of the capital, Akbar wishes not merely to travel to meet the enemy but to engage in a more thrilling kind of travel, a voyage of the mind and heart. He wants to be transported. Carol Sicherman remarks :

> In this kind of 'transport', a spiritual and intellectual ecstasy, individual identity is expanded, translated, so that multiple entities coexist in a single consciousness. Mukherjee herself is a translated person ... Mukherjee's fiction translates Indian and Western cultures into one another.[10]

"Courtly Vision" invites us to look back on *Darkness* and to observe the multiple perspectives of Western and Indian art, to see how Mukherjee herself has accommodated a decidedly Hindu imagination with an Americanized sense of the craft of fiction. Perhaps the best way of penetrating *Darkness* is to understand it as another work in the spirit of Akbar, tolerant of diversity while seeking unity of vision. As Akbar was a conqueror and a syncretist, hoping to create a new vision out of elements of previous ideas, so Mukherjee's 'insurrections of language, (her) subversions or deliberate destructions of sacrosanct literary forms,' aim at creating new vision. In *Darkness* she charts the territory to be conquered, territory worthy of 'epic' treatment in some future maximalist fiction. The final command that she attributes to Emperor Akbar sums up her own effort as an artist : "Transport me... into the hearts of men."

Bharati Mukherjee's other collection of short stories, the winner of the National Book Critics Circle Award, *The Middleman and Other Stories* (1988) marks an advance over her previous collection (*Darkness*) in that its scope is broader, vision more perceptive and language more Americanised. It portrays the experiences of immigrants from Europe, the Caribbean, and other parts of Asia as well as India in the USA. In *Darkness* Mukherjee drew her characters from many subcontinental classes and religions. In *The Middleman*, she goes even further, gathering protagonists from all over the globe sometime she leaves out the Indians altogether. Commenting on the thematic content of these stories Gomez perceptively remarks :

> The theme of these stories is immigration and the reciprocal effect of the immigrants and American life on each other. In these stories which deal with energetic immigrants, there is a definite movement away from expatriates who were marginal men and women to immigrants who are middlemen in more sense than one. They are not only brokers or go betweens in various deals, but people who are in the middle of where action is.[11]

Mukherjee, herself is a middleman here, an interpreter between two cultures. She is grappling with big subjects such as violence, culture shock, politics not always with equal success. But the writing remains elegant and economical. She tells Carb in an interview :

> The new, changing America is the theme of the stories in *The Middleman*. For me, immigration from the Third World to this country is a metaphor for the process of uprooting and re-rooting, or what my husband Clark Blaise in his book *Resident Alien* calls "unhousement" and "rehousement." The immigrants in my stories go through extreme transformations in America and at the same time they alter the country's appearance and psychological make-up. In some ways, they are like

> European immigrants of earlier eras. But they have different gods. And they come from different regions.[12]

She explores the American experience through various personae or protagonists, four of whom are white American males, six of them are females (only three of the women are of Indian origin). The result is a curious mix of voices and experiences that go to make up the celebration of being American (as she states in *Darkness*) as opposed to being Canadian. Most of the stories are monologues, spoken by compulsively fluent talkers whose lives are too urgent and mobile for them to indulge in the luxury of the retrospective past tense. They hit the page in full flight and move through the world at speed with the reader straining to keep at speed with them. Every story ends on a new point of departure. Raban asserts, "people are last seen walking out through an open door, planning an escape or suspended on the optimistic brink of blissful sexual transport."[13] Possibly the greatest tribute to *The Middleman And Other Stories*, came from American critics who were very enthusiastic in their appraisal of the book. Among them the most glaring comment comes from John Coates :

> What was the greatest American novel supposed to do, back in the days when we still believed in it, if it was to take some kind of a definitive measure of our collective character, then Bharati Mukherjee has come closer to that goal with this book of stories.[14]

The Middleman is about the experience of eleven people who have deliberately chosen to make America their new home not because of some political unrest upsetting their lives in their native lands, but out of lure for a better life, they have drifted themselves into a situation. Thus, the book does not focus exclusively on the Indian experience but details the lives of other immigrants — Hispanics, Italians and Sri Lankans as well. These characters from different backgrounds are forced to make their individual cultures take a back seat as they are busy absorbing the American milieu. Every now and then the native flavour peeps through this special American cover. Besides adjustment syndrome, the baser sides of American life, its license of violence takes a strong grip over these immigrants, leaving them in a mess. The basic theme of all these stories therefore becomes the struggle that the unfortunate immigrants have to encounter and the anguish they have to undergo in the process of adjusting themselves and earning a livelihood. "Despite this incisive understanding of the immigrant dilemma, Bharati Mukherjee, does not believe in working out a satisfactory solution to this problem in the case of her characters. They are left in their grove, like cast away for whom there is no hope."[15] Cultural fusion is possible, to some extent, but transfer of cultures is not possible. For assimilation it is imperative that one should keep his harrowing past at a distance but it is humanly impossible. Polly Shulman also subscribes to this view :

> Assimilation implies forgetting, blotting out the past, but the past is what the present is made of. If she weren't still an Indian, Mukherjee wouldn't be the wonderful American writer she is.[16]

The title story *The Middleman* narrates the experiences of Alfie Judah, a hustler of Middle Eastern Jewish descent. It is a first person narrative. He quite humorously talks about his adventures before coming to America. He is a widely travelled person who has come across several misadventures. As he himself confides :

> I've seen worse. I've seen Baghdad, Bombay, Queens — and now this moldering spread deep in Mayan country. Aztecs, Toltecs, mestizos, even some bashful whites with German accents. All that and a lot of Texans, I'll learn the ropes.[17]

Presently he works as a middleman and earns his living "from things that fall" (p. 3). He supplies guns to guerrillas in Mayan Country.

Bharati Mukherjee tells Sibyl Steinberg in an interview about the origin of this title story. It came about because "I happened to be in Costa Rica at the time when American and Central American history was being made."[18] In another interview she explains the inspiration behind the book :

> It grew out of an incomplete novel about a man who served in the army in Vietnam, and who, after the war, becomes a professional soldier and hires himself out in Afghanistan and Central America. While I was working on that novel, a character with a minor role, a Jew has

> relocated from Baghdad to Bombay to Brooklyn, took control and wrote his own story. He attracted me because he was a cynical person and a hustler, as many immigrant survivors have to be. So Alfie Judah, the protagonist in the Middleman, travels around the world, providing people with what they need, guns, narcotics, automobiles. The story takes place in an unnamed country in Central America where he becomes involved in a Guerrilla war.[19]

Alfie Judah is an interesting person. He does not hide anything from us and confesses even his greatest weaknesses : "I must confess my weakness. It's woman" (p. 4). His history is that of an uprooted person. He has been forced to do works that are illegal and dangerous. His present citizenship is also always in jeopardy and his "dealings can't stand too much investigation" (p. 5). Though he regrets "There are aspects of American life I came too late for and will never understand" (p. 5) still he is a fighter to the core who does everything for his survival. He is a middleman in two senses — in his profession and in his life also. He has connection with underworld and supplies them arms and immunition, thus working as a middleman between the manufacturer and buyers of the war material. At the same time, he is used by his master T. Ransome as a middleman between his wife Maria and her lover Bud. Because "Clovis (Ransome) wanted a cut of Bud's action. But Bud refused and that got Clovis mad. Clovis even offered money, but Bud said no way. Clovis pushed me on him, so he took but he still didn't budge" (p. 16).

As a result of this Maria starts loving Alfie who is not very enthusiastic in his response because the ghost of past always haunts him. He cannot forget his Iraqi experience where he had seen "A young woman, possibly adulterous but certainly bold and brave and beautiful enough to excite rumors of promiscuity, was stoned to death" (p. 7). Thus he is among those very few Americans who know the sound of rocks cutting through flesh and striking bone. One of the few to count the costs of adultery. At the end of the story Alfie's client Clovis is killed by one of the guerrillas, a friend of his wife and Alfie is spared because once the girl had loved him. He plans a retreat to the nearest town contemplating "There must be something worth trading in the troubles I have seen" (p. 21).

Most probably he wishes to sell the information about guerrillas to the concerned authorities. Thus he is a real middleman, cunning, opportunistic and adaptive. Thus the story reveals the hazards of survival for an immigrant in America with its inherent message that only those can survive who have determination and toughness of mind who can snatch opportunities out of turmoil.

The other three stories — "A Wife's Story," "The Tenant" and "Jasmine" — each with a female protagonist from the Third World, illustrate the author's technique and her success in conveying the theme of rebirth or refashioning of the self by immigrant experience. In each of them we encounter a different woman at a different stage in the subtle, complex, and traumatic process of becoming a new woman, one who is at home in the sometimes terrifying freedom of the new American culture. In each story, the exhilarating sense of possibility clashes with the debilitating sense of loss, yet the exuberant determination of the women attracts us to them and denies the power of pity. "A Wife's Story" is a very powerful manifestation of the survival instinct of an Indian woman. The protagonist here is an Indian Patel, Mrs. Panna Bhatt, who goes to America for taking a Ph.D. degree without her husband who works in India. She is a survivor and adapter who can find the true meaning of her life by 'refashioning' herself according to demands of America. She knows that to survive in America she should have to break taboos and to walk out of the confines of a traditional role model Indian wife.

An Indian wife can never think of making someone her friend who is married to somebody else because she knows that even a memory of others is a sign of disloyalty. But here is a woman who has befriended Imre, a Hungarian fellow who has left his wife and two sons back home. Again Mukherjee has used the technique of first person narrative. Panna has adapted herself so well to the social and cultural milieu of America that she feels 'light' almost 'free'. She is conscious of her achievement which is in striking contrast to her mother's and grandmother's. She knows that she has made something meaningful of her passive Indian wife's existence. She has endeavoured the American experience which has made her more confident, more self-reliant and more meaningful. As she boasts :

> Memories of Indian destitutes mix with the hordes of New York steel people, and they float free, like astronauts, inside my head. I've made it. I'm making something of my life (p. 29).

In a delightfully conversational tone she brings out the obvious contrast between her situation and that of her mother and grandmother :

> My mother was beaten by her mother-in-law, my grandmother, when she'd registered for French lessons at the Alliance Francaise. My grandmother, the eldest daughter of a rich Zamindar, was illiterate (p. 29).

Panna is the one who boldly expedited the experience of being an American. But her Indian sense of pride cannot tolerate the vulgar comment of players of a David Mamet play (Glengarry Glen Ross) about Indian women : "There women... they look like they've just been fucked by a dead cat" (p. 26). This comment is enough to upset her nerves "Tears come : I want to stand, scream, make an awful scene. I long for ugly, nasty rage" (p. 26). Actually her rage is not against Mamet's play, she raises a voice of protest against the tyranny of American dream. As she says :

> I don't hate Mamet. It's the tyranny of the American dream that scares me. First, you don't exist. Then you're invisible. Then you're funny. Then you're disgusting. Insult, my American friends will tell me, is a kind of acceptance. No instant dignity here. A play like this, back home, would cause riots, communal, racists, and antisocial (p. 26).

Panna is a product of post colonial situation. Had she been born in Colonial India she would not have resented. She should have calmly accepted this as her fate. But post coloniality has given her a 'green card,' now she is free to exercise her mind, her power of reasoning, her sense of pride and dignity anywhere in the world. As she claims : "Post-colonialism has made me their referee. It's hate I long for; simple, brutish, partisan hate" (p. 27).

For survival in America the immigrants have to go through all kinds of trials and tribulations. They have to seal their hearts. They have to forgo all sense of morality, decency and decorum. This is the case of Charity Chin, an "Oriental" model and Panna's roommate. "She had her eyes fixed eight or nine months ago and out of gratitude sleeps with her plastic surgeon every third Wednesday" (p. 29). Panna is aware of the fact that to get something one must pay. She promptly claims : "If I hadn't left home, I'd never have heard of the Wuchang Uprising. I've broadened my horizons" (p. 31). But this bold experimentor and an astronaut flying in the American space, has not left her life as an Indian wife altogether. As soon as she receives the message of her husband's arrival she adopts the form of an Indian wife :

> I change out of cotton pants and shirt I've been wearing all day and put on a sari to meet my husband at JFK. I don't forget the jewellery; the marriage necklace of 'mangalsutra', gold drop ear-rings, heavy gold bangles. I don't wear them everyday (p. 33).

The above statement of Panna is ironical because we know that underneath the familiar costume she is not the same woman. She is not sure whether she is unhappy about it. Her adaptability is contrasted with her husband's mental block when he visits America. The husband is put off by the too friendly attitude of Lebanese towards his wife at the counter. The utter informality of the guide (who even sings a song) is disgusting for him.

Panna is heavily weighed down by the burdens of two cultures and she has to bear the hardships of trying to balance parts of her old life with the best of the new. She mutters : "Tonight I should make up to him for my years away, the gutted trucks, the degree I'll never use in India. I want to pretend with him (the husband) that nothing has changed" (p. 40). The end of the story encapsulates both the strength of her spirited struggle to refashion herself and the difficulty of achieving wholeness when one is stretched between two cultures.

Maya Sanyal, the female protagonist of the story "The Tenant" is shocked when her landlord lover refers to the two of them as "two wounded people," (p. 112) and thinks about herself that "she knows she is strange, and lonely, but being Indian is not the same. She would have thought, as being a freak" (p. 112). Maya Sanyal, the central figure of the story, recognizes her strangeness in America and her appalling loneliness, but she resists being recognized as a "freak." No doubt, this term occurs to her when her current lover, Fred, a man without arms, refers to them both as wounded. She does not see herself as being as freakish as Fred, as bereft as Fred, though certainly the story makes clear that she has been wounded emotionally and spiritually by the struggle to come to terms with her new life in America. In one sense, Fred's assessment is accurate, for as the author indicates in all the stories in this collection, it is impossible to adapt to life in the New World without inflicting some kind of injury to one's spirit.

It is apparently a deeper wound for the women of the Third World, who are engaged in the struggle to achieve a new identity for themselves in an alien culture. Perhaps this struggle results from their sudden freedom from the bonds of superstition and chauvinism that held them fast in their old, familiar cultures, freedom that seems to leave them floating; unbalanced, in the complex, sometimes treacherous air of this new and unfamiliar culture. The irony is that this refashioning of the self is both painful and exhilarating. In an interview, Mukherjee asserts :

> We immigrants have fascinating tales to relate. Many of us have lived in newly independent or emerging countries which are plagued by civil and religious conflicts. We have experienced rapid changes in the history of the nations in which we lived. When we uproot ourselves from those countries and come here, either by choice or out of necessity, we suddenly must absorb 200 years of American history and learn to adapt to American society. Our lives are remarkable often heroic.[20]

Mukherjee illustrates this heroic quality through her characters who are filled with a hustlerish kind of energy, and more importantly,

> they take risks they wouldn't have taken in their old, comfortable worlds to solve their problems. As they change citizenship, they are reborn.[21]

In the other story "The Tenant", we first meet the protagonist, Maya, sitting over a glass of bourbon (the first one of her life) with a new colleague from the new job in the English Department at the University of Northern Iowa. The American colleague, Fran, is on the Hiring, Tenure, and Reappointment Committee and is partly responsible for bringing Maya to the school. While Fran chats about her own life and gossips a little about Maya's landlord, Maya contemplates the immensity of her isolation and loneliness. Although she longs to confide in someone, Fran even, she realizes that he is unable to receive these confidences because Fran cannot see that Maya is a woman caught in the mingled web of two very different cultures. To Fran, "a utopian and feminist" (p. 100), Maya is a bold adventurer who has made a clean break with her Indian past, but Maya understands, that there is no such thing as a "clean" break.

When Maya is invited to a Sunday afternoon tea by another Bengali, Dr. Rabindra Chatterji, a Professor of Physics in her new university, she accepts the proposal with somewhat mixed feelings but dresses carefully in one of her best and loveliest saris. Once inside Chatterjee's house, in a raw suburban development that seems full of other Third World nationalities, Maya allows the familiar sights and smells to Indian high tea to take her back to that other world of "Brahminness." Maya's hostess begins to ask questions about her illustrious family in Calcutta, and Maya thinks herself that "nothing in Calcutta is ever lost" (p. 104). Apparently the story of her "indiscretions" with various men, her marriage and divorce to an American, is known to the entire Bengali community in North America. She has been marked as a "loose" woman and as a divorcee, and therefore cannot ever hope to remarry respectably in the Indian community. Dr. Chatterji is easily infatuated by her personality. He feels so excited that he starts masturbating in his car when he goes to see her off. His pain of suppressed desire comes out when he says :

> Divorced women can date, they can go to bars and discos. They can see mens, many mens. But inside marriage there is so much loneliness (p. 108).

She is aware :

> Indian men want Indian brides. Married Indian men want Indian mistresses. All over America, "handsome, tall, fair" engineers, doctors, data processors — the new pioneers — cry their eerie love calls (p. 109).

Maya is a typical immigrant who has been wandering through many places : Calcutta, North Carolina, New Jersey and finally Iowa, has indulged in sexual encounters with many persons she "has slept with married men, with nameless men, with men little more than boys" (p. 103). She has never slept with an Indian man and now she madly wants to do so and responds promptly to a dubious personal ad in the immigrant Indian Weekly. She locates her male counterpart in Ashok Mehta, a sexually liberated professional also divided between romantic love and sexual promiscuity. At the end of the story, after their courtship has entered its final phase, and she has decided to go to Connecticut to be with him, she finally repudiates her own accusations that her life is grim and perverse, that "She has changed her citizenship, but she hasn't broken through into the light, the vigour, the bustle of the New World" (p. 110). At the end she does bustle off to meet the man who will make her whole again in this new life. Thus Maya is always on the move and makes an anarchy of her life to find the real sense of belonging, the real sense of "wholeness" and "fulfilment" in her life. Divided between cultures, Maya the eternal enchantress, corrupts the ethos of both East and West. She remains neither an American nor an Indian. She is hanging in the air like the mythical 'Trishanku,' and typifies the real condition of a person caught in the net of two cultures.

The next story, "Jasmine," also explores some of the more appalling and grotesque aspects of the cultural collisions. In this story, the protagonist is a young Trinidadian woman named Jasmine who has been smuggled illegally into the United States, all paid for by her father. She knew "she'd outsmarted the guys at the border," now it was upto her to use her wits to do something with her life. As her Daddy kept saying, "Girl, is opportunity come only once" (p. 128) she realises that her 'resourcefulness of inventiveness are indispensable tools for survival and success'. Jasmine is proud of her family in Port-of-Spain but she is an ardent explorer who has come to America by choice and so for her being nobody in America is better than being somebody in Trinidad. Here she is free to trace her new identity because "who would know in Detroit that she was Dr. Vassanji's daughter?"

First of all Jasmine starts working for her fellow Trinidadians the Daboos. She is an intelligent girl who has come to America for making something of her life. She is ardent and laborious and on Sunday mornings she helps unload packing crates of Caribbean spices in a shop on the next block. "This was a new life, and she wanted to learn everything" (p. 129). One of the first things that she learned was that 'Ann Arbor was a magic world ... Ann Arbor was the place to be' (p. 129). She manages to move to Ann Arbor and "That evening she had a job with the Moffits. Bill Moffit taught molecular biology and Lara Hatch Moffit, his wife, was a performance artist.... The Moffits had a little girl, Muffin, whom Jasmine was to look after" (p. 131). Thus, it is the beginning of a new life as an au-pair for Jasmine and she is all ecstatic about it. "Jasmine knew she was lucky to have found a small, clean, friendly family like the Moffits to build her new life around" (p. 134). Jasmine is intelligent enough to notice the differences between her world and that of the Americans. As we see her muttering "This wasn't the time to say anything about Ram, the family servant. Americans like the Moffits wouldn't understand about keeping servants" (p. 131). She is afraid that Bill may ask her about her visa or green card number and social security but to her satisfaction "all Bill did was smile and smile at her" (p. 132) and nothing else. Instead of Bill

> Lara asked about Port-of-Spain. There was nothing to tell about her hometown that wouldn't shame her in front of nice white Amereican folk like the Moffits. The place was shabby, the people were grasping and cheating and lying and life was full of despair and drink and wanting (p. 132).

Jasmine soon realizes that things are 'topsy-turvy' in Moffits household because 'Lara went on two and three days road trips and Bill stayed home' (p. 133). Jasmine is surprised to see Bill cooking, a professor doing this without "getting paid to do it". It also surprises her "The Moffits didn't go to church, though they seemed to be good Christians. They just didn't talk church talk" (p. 133). At times Jasmine suffers feats of nostalgia but even then there is no looking back for her. She has herself chosen to be where she is. Lara often visits far off places for her performances and she is left alone in the house with Bill and Moffin, the daughter. "Bill, Muffie, and she were a family, almost" (p. 136). She starts loving Bill. He comes 'barging into her dreams in his funny, loose-jointed, clumsy way' (p. 136). Bill has also fallen in love with her. "You feel so good," he said, "You smell so good. You're really something, flower of Trinidad." At this she replies "Flower of Ann Arbor, not Trinidad" (p. 138). This makes it amply clear that she has developed a sense of belonging. The story culminates with her seduction by her master on the same Turkish carpet which she used to clean everyday. The whole description shows that she has no moral scruples as such :

> She felt so good she was dizzy. She'd never felt this good on the island where men did this all the time, and girls went along with it always for favours. You couldn't feel really good in a nothing place. She was thinking this as they made love on the Turkish carpet in front of the fire : she was a bright, pretty girl with no visa, no papers, and no birth certificate. No nothing other than what she wanted to invent and tell. She was a girl rushing wildly into the future (p. 138).

Thus we see that Jasmine is an adventurer, ready to pay the price for realizing her American dream. Such was the charm of this character that later Mukherjee made her the heroine of the next novel, *Jasmine* (1989). The story runs on the same line in the novel with slight differences. Jasmine in the novel comes from India not from Trinidad and shows the same zeal for absorption in the mainstream American culture.

In the story titled "Loose Ends," a Vietnam Vet, who is working in Miami as a hired killer describes the details of his job with off hand boredom, while his attention is fully engaged by the sight of a blond Swami levitating on a prayer mat above the roof of a discount clothing store in the suburban shopping mall. Airborne for two or three minutes, the flying Swami is eventually caught by the police in a safety net and hauled off to jail. The whole incident is over and done within seven short sentences but it haunts the book.

The protagonists feel a certain kind of hollowness within them in Mukherjee's stories. Inspite of love there is no fulfilment, the lovers feel alienated. There is no real communication between them. Jeb and Jonda have been living together yet the bond between them has not been established. Jeb confesses :

> I get in bed with her. Usually afternoons are pure dynamite, when I can get them. I lie down with her for a while, but nothing happens (p. 44).

Jonda's anguish is also noteworthy :

> Nine years, for God's sake! Nine years, and what do we have?

There is no real relationship. "What we have sounds like the Constitution of the United States. We have freedom and no strings attached. We have no doubts. We come and go as we like" (p. 45).

Jeb has not forgotten his misadventures of twenty years ago. His past haunts his present like a ghost :

> Twenty years ago I missed the meaning of things around me. I was seventeen years old, in Heidelberg, Germany, about to be shipped out to Vietnam. We had guys on the base selling passages to Sweden. And I had a week end pass and a free flight to London. Held them in my hand : Sweden forever, or a weekend pass. Wise up, Kid, choose life, whispered the cook, a twenty year lifer with a quarter million stashed in Arizona. Seventeen years old and guys are offering me life or death (pp. 48-49).

Next he went to London 'a kid checking out the snakes and gators of my childhood' in a zoo. "That snake-shit — all that coiled power — stays with me, always. That's what happened to us in the paddy fields. We drowned in our shit. An inscrutable humanoid python sleeping on a bed of turds : that's what I never want to be" (p. 49). But the irony of fate is that "This is what I've become. I want to squeeze this state dry and swallow it whole" (p. 54). Jeb is an immigrant and like other immigrants he also has a survival instinct. Doc Healy's caution words "If you want to stay alive just keep consuming and moving like a locust. Do that, Jeb m'boy, and you'll survive to die a natural death" (p. 45) fills him with confidence in this new world.

"Loose Ends" tests the responses of white Americans to immigrants. Marshall, an American, is hurt when his Filipino girl friend, Blanquita leaves him but quickly takes another woman to assuage his loneliness. When Blanquita has a change of heart, Marshal is prepared to take her back. Thus Marshall's acceptance of Blanquita's foreignness and his feelings surmount the cultural gap between them.

The next story "Orbiting" is really in the orbit of the book. It is one of the most successful stories in the anthology. It records an awkward, subversively joyous Thanksgiving Day dinner that is used by an Italian-American girl as an occasion for introducing her Afghan lover to her family. Here we see the cultural confusion resulting from the encounter of immigrants from two different continents. It is a first person narrative in which Renata, an Italian American girl narrates the whole affair half wittingly, half-seriously. She belongs to the third generation of immigrants and for her Italianness is now a metaphor. Renata is her Italian name, now she is Rindy. She had formerly been in love with Vic but he left her saying :

> I'm leaving babe. New Jersey doesn't do it for me anymore (p. 62).

Her present lover is 'Ro' — Roashan from Kabul, he fled from there "to take classes at NJIT and become an electrical engineer" (p. 64). He is exotic for Rindy as she claims : "He's totally unlike any man I have ever known... He comes from a macho culture" (p. 65). 'Ro' has changed her entire perception about America.

> When I'm with Ro I feel I am looking at America through the wrong end of telescope. He makes it sound like a police State, with sudden raids, papers, detention centres, deportations, and torture and death waiting in wings (p. 66).

Because this is the fate of the newly migrated people in America. 'Ro' comes from a 'culture of pain.'

> The skin on his back is speckled and lumpy from burns, but when I ask he laughs. A crazy villager whacked him with a burning stick for cheekiness, he explains. He's

> ashamed that he comes from a culture of pain. 'Ro' reveals he was tortured in jail ... Electrodes, canes, freezing tanks. He leaves nothing out (p. 73).

He lays bare the condition of such people who migrate to USA or such countries because of civil strife in their country. "Colombo, Seoul, Bombay, Geneva, Frankfurt, I know too well the transit lounges of many airports. We travel the world with our gym bags and prayer rugs, unrolling them in the transit lounges" (p. 73).

The well settled Italian-American father of Rindy can never take a man like 'Ro' to be a fit guy for Rindy. He is gravely mistaken by him when he enters the house unknocked. Rindy's father takes him for one of the refugees in the famine camp and assures him "You won't starve this afternoon" (p. 68). He is different. His manners are mistaken for timidity. For Rindy's Dad and Brent "Even his head-sake is foreign" (p. 71), but Rindy has no problem. She knows "Each culture establishes its own manly posture, different ways of claiming space" (p. 70). She loves his emotionality, his way of appreciating her as she sincerely confesses :

> I realize all in a rush how much I love this man with his blemished, tortured body ... Ro's my chance to heal the world (p. 74).

And now she vows :

> I shall teach him how to walk like an American, how to dress like Brent but better, how to fill up room as Dad does instead of melting and blending but sticking out in the Afghan way (pp. 74-75).

Thus here we see how the native Americans have made a space for the new settlers. Rindy is American and by adopting 'Ro' as her lover she embraces an exotic immigrant and thinks it her duty to Americanize him so that he can survive there.

"Fighting For the Rebound" is yet another story dealing with the problem of immigration. It is a first person narrative and we come to see the story of a young aristocrate immigrant from Asia, from the point of view of a native American. Blanquita, the protagonist is from Philippines. She 'speaks six languages, her best being Tagalog, Spanish and American ... Back in Manila, she took a crash course in making nice to Americans' (p. 79). She struggles to succeed in the American society but at the same time she is conscious of the trauma involved. "I should never have left Manila. Pappy was right. The East is East and the West is West and never the twain shall meet" (p. 80). She is aware of the difference of cultures. She has made a brave attempt to adapt herself and liked to believe as though real life began for her at JKF when she got past the customs and immigration on the seventeenth of October 1980.

Her relationship keeps on breaking continuously because the institution of marriage holds no water in America. Young couples prefer the 'live-in' style where sex is the ephemeral bond. Real happiness eludes American society because human relations are based less on mutual love and trust. Hence, there is constant breaking away from each other which puts American social fabric under stress. Young immigrants like Blanquita are caught in the web of sexual freedom in the name of liberation in desperate attempts to succeed in the United States.

Griff and Blanquita, too, go through the process of breaking up. Griff, the narrator, is keen to save his relationship with Blanquita and proposes to her truce. But her complain rings strident, 'You don't love me Griff' (p. 82). He is reminded of his previous relationship breaking with Wendi, 'We walked, we did thing together', but it all ended'. The story appears to be repeating with Blanquita also. Pathetically Griff sums it up "Love frees, but we are stuck with love's debris" (p. 82), and Blanquita shouts at him :

> Not just you Griff ... you're all emotional cripples. All you Americans. You just worry about your own meshy little relationships. You don't care how much you hurt the world (p. 85).

This is the typical response of a woman from the Eastern world to the 'emotionless,' 'soulless' practicality of the American culture. It is enough to upset the nerves of Blanquita. "I can't stand it anymore, Griff. It's got to stop" (p. 85), she cries. Thus, here one notices that an immigrant's story is not always one of success and it is full of pain and anguish as it happens with Blanquita.

In "Fathering," Eng, a Vietnamese child, rescued by her American father from Saigon, is brought home. The father Jason is narrating the whole thing :

> Vietnam didn't happen, and I'd put it behind me in marriage and fatherhood and teaching high school .... Until Eng popped up in my life, I really believed it didn't happen (p. 118).

Jase, the Vietnam Vet, is the middleman caught between his American girl friend Sharon and his Vietnamese daughter Eng, between the pills and tranquilizers of Western medicine and the curse little Eng believes in. He notices a change in the behaviour of his girl friend who does not feel easy with the Saigon Kid Eng :

> Once upon a time Sharon used to be cheerful, accommodating woman. It is n't as if Eng was dumped on us out of the blue. She knew I was tracking my kid. Coming to terms with the past was Sharon's idea. I don't know what happened to that Sharon (p. 118).

The child is laid with high fever and comes to their bedroom door saying : "I'm hungry, Dad..., let's go down to kitchen. Just you and me" (p. 118). Noticing Sharon moving her body in the bed, she quickly adds, "Not her, Dad. We don't want her with us in the kitchen" (p. 119). Jasc trics to explain the situation to Sharon, "Love not spite — makes Eng so territorial; that's what I want to explain to Sharon. She's sick, frightened, foreign kid, for Chrissake" (p. 119). But this is not enough to appease her. She retorts immediately : "You know what's wrong with you Jase? You can't admit you're being manipulated. You can't cut through the frightened-foreign-kid Shit" (p. 119). She accuses Eng of spoiling her happy world :

> Everything was fine until she got here. Send her back Jase. If you love, send her back (p. 123).

Sharon is looking helpless and pathetic and Jase is filled with 'guilt' not 'love' for her. The torn lover tries to comfort his girl friend but it all turns out to be futile. A psychiatrist hands a tranquilizer to the child (Eng). Eng screams : 'Get the hell out, you bastard! ... When they shoot my grandama, you think pills do her any good?' (p. 124).

Thus the dilemma of Jase is the dilemma of all the immigrants who are caught between the promises of the New World and the bruises of the old one. Jase's failure at bringing about any kind of reconciliation between his American girl friend and Vietnamese daughter confirms the fact that reconciliation between the two cultures is not possible. In no way an oppressor and an oppressed can be friends. 'Blood is thicker' and so at last we see Jase moving with his daughter :

> My Saigon kid and me : we're a team. In five minutes we'll be safely away in the cold chariot of our van (p. 124).

As a contrast to the educated, upper middle class Indian immigrants, Mukherjee creates the wily Danny Sahib, in her story "Danny's Girls," who procures Indian mail order brides in a New York ghetto. The narrator here is a teenager of Indian origin who has never visited India. He discloses the real identity of Danny "Aunt Lini still called him Dinesh, the name he'd landed with. He was about twenty, a Dogra boy from Simla.... He wasn't an enforcer, he was a charmer. No one was afraid of him, he was a merchant of opportunity" (p. 141). He works for Danny Sahib. Danny Sahib was in marriage-market racket :

> The real money wasn't in rupees and bringing saps over. It was in selling docile Indian girls to hard up Americans for real bucks. An Old World wife who knew her place and would breed like crazy was at least twenty thousand dollars .... My job was to put up posters in landromats and pass out flyers on the subways (p. 143).

Here Bharati Mukherjee contrasts between the job he is doing to his dreams, that he wouldn't disclose to his beloved, the most beautiful girl in Aunt Lini's pet-shop :

> What I wanted to be in those days was someone important, which meant a freedom like Danny's but without the scams. Respectable freedom in the bigger world of America, that's what I wanted... I would be going to Columbia University to the Engineering school ... I

> didn't want to turn out like my Aunt Lini, ghetto moneylender, and I didn't want to suffer like my mother, and I hated my father with a passion (pp. 44-45).

But the dreams remain simple dreams. His attempt to find a true identity in a foreign culture through entering Columbia University remains a distant dream. Now the only dream he cherishes is to free himself and Rosie from the clutches of Danny. Danny bullies him by saying a 'hijra' and his manliness comes to the fore. "How dare he call me a 'hijra,' eunuch?" (p. 148) He can overcome this insult only by getting his Rosie by his side. 'The first I felt my life was going to be A-Okay' (p. 149) with this realization of the narrator the story ends. Thus Mukherjee focuses here on the paradoxes of the life of immigrants — what they want to be and what they become — they have no will of their own.

"Buried Lives" (significantly named after a Matthew Arnold poem of the same name) tells us in a comic mode the quest for identity of a Tamil School teacher from Sri Lanka, Mr. N.K.S. Venkateshan. The protagonist leads a buried life, 'living and partly living', explicating Arnold's "The Buried Life" inside a St. Joseph's Collegiate classroom. Bharati Mukherjee explains why Mr. Venkatesan, to whom nothing seems to happen and who is not a political man, suddenly finds himself caught in the vortex of political activity released by Tamil Liberation Tigers :

> Mr. Venkatesan ... had a large family to look after : he had parents, one set of grandparents, an aunt who hadn't been quite right in the head since four or five boy had signed up with the Tigers, and three much younger sisters. They lived with him in a three-room flat... It was to protect his younger sister that he was marching that afternoon with two hundred baby-faced protesters (p. 154).

He accidently injures (though he thinks he kills) a Home Guard Officer with an axe and life is not the same after that :

> Months later, in a boarding house, in Hamburg, Mr. Venkatesan couldn't help thinking about the flock of young monks pressed together behind a police barricade that eventful afternoon (p. 156).

He owes his freedom to the monks who compelled him to leave Sri Lanka. Like the Gloucester sub-plot in *King Lear* Mukherjee sets up her two parallel quests : the forty-nine year old school teacher's thirst for freedom is counter-pointed against that of his sister. From a pliant plain girl she had changed into a fanatic revolutionary, ferociously in love with a Tiger, "Something harse and womanly seemed to be happening inside her" (p. 155). It is a kind of metamorphosis, creation of a new identity for her. In his quest for freedom and a fresh identity, Mr. Venkatesan thinks of emigrating. "But every country he could see himself being happy and fulfilled inturned him down" (p. 160). But the force that drives him once again comes from his sister's example :

> She'd meant to leave home, with or without his permission. She'd freed herself of family duties and bonds (p. 163).

In other words she had found her true identity and acts as a catalyst for the protagonist's severing all bonds, finding his true identity. All his life he has dutifully lived for others and now he wants to live his own life. And so on to Hamburg, a launching pad for Canada.

Mr. Venkatesan like other immigrants makes a brave attempt to reach USA via India, Russia and Europe. In the way he happens to meet Queenie, a widow and falls in love with her. In the way, he was made to adjust in a 'smallish attic room with unventillated smoke, fitted with two sets of three tier bunks.' He had four other young men--Asia and Africa were their continents sharing his small room, with whom he had nothing in common 'except waiting.' An immigrant, 'without papers accepts last minute humiliations,' Mr. Venkatesan knows this. Everything is right till Queenie's daughter steals travel documents of the inmates and Lubee calls the police to hand over the illegal. Mr. Venkatesan regrets, "he had started out as a teacher and a solid citizen and end up a lusty criminal" (p. 175). But at this juncture Queenie, the deliverer of radiant dreams, burst through the door of the Kitchen. "Leave him alone!" She yelled to the man from Lubec. "You're harrassing my fiance! He's a future German citizen. He will become my husband" (p. 176).

What is significant to note here is Bharati Mukherjee's message that inspite of having made momentuous filial sacrifices, spending hard earned money, endangering one's life all along the passage to reach the United States, one doesn't always make it. He falls short of its end, if not its goal, and the dream remains unfulfilled.

The concluding piece of the collection "The Management of Grief" is a quietly stunning story dramatizing the imagined consequences of a plane crash that actually occurred a couple of years ago and forms the content of her *The Sorrow and Terror : The Haunting Legacy of Air India Tragedy*. An Air India jet enroute Canada exploded over the sea off the West Coast of Ireland; sabotage was suspected. Mukherjee is remarkably perceptive about the effects of the disaster on the victims' relatives in Canada : the isolation and withdrawal of these Indian families, despite clumsy official efforts to help them, and the varying degrees to which they were able to adapt.

This story is not one of celebration but of bereavement. Mrs. Bhave makes a brave effort to cope with the loss of her husband and two sons killed in an air crash. It was suspected that it was an act of terrorism by Sikh militants. People have been muttering 'Sikh bomb, Sikh bomb. The men, not using the word, bow their head in agreement' (pp. 179-180). There is no hysteria but 'calm,' just a deadening quiet. A lot of immigrants, mainly Indians have lost their family members in this tragedy. Rather than the narrator, it is the people she encounters, the Irish authorities and the policemen who cannot control their feelings :

> The Irish are not shy, they rush to me and give me hugs and some are crying. I cannot imagine reactions like that on the streets of Toronto. Just strangers, and I am touched. Some carry flowers with them and give them to any Indian they see (p. 187).

The writer does not focus on the sensationalism, ethics and the politics of the disaster, rather draws out the story to reflect on the ensuing years, to bring out the dead weight of a lone survivor's wife. Mrs. Bhave goes to her parents in India after the tragedy where the mother pleads to her to "stay longer, Canada is a cold place. Why would you want to be all yourself" (p. 189). She decides to stay on. During a visit to a Sadhu she had a vision of her deceased husband, whom she asked, "Shall I stay... He only smiles, you must finish alone what we started together" (p. 190). Hence, she returns. She looks calm and quiet in her reactions. She does not scream. She herself confesses :

> I was always controlled, but never repressed. Sound can reach me, but my body is tensed, ready to scream. I hear their voices all around me. I hear my boys and Vikram cry, "Mummy, Shaila!" and their screams insulate me, like head phones (p. 180).

She repents her reluctance :

> I never once told him (her husband) that I loved him... I was so well brought up I never felt comfortable calling my husband by his first name (p. 181).

Judith Templeton, the social worker comes to her for support in rescue operations because she is 'a pillar.' She has taken the tragedy 'more calmly'. Judith fails to see beneath the skin. Shaila cannot tell her though she wants to say : "I want to say her, I wish I could scream, starve, walk into Lake Ontario, jump from a bridge... I am a freak. No one who has ever known me would think of me reacting this way. This terrible calm will not go away" (p. 183). The thing is that she is caught between two worlds. "I am trapped between two modes of knowledge. At thirty-six I am too old to start over and too young to give up. Like my husband's spirit, I flutter between worlds" (p. 189). But the fact is that "we must all grieve in our own way" (p. 183). Kusum, another widow has withdrawn from her surviving daughter and the world and finds solace in an Ashram at Hardwar. Another aggrieved 'Dr. Ranganathan from Montreal... has lost a huge family, something indescribable.' Now for him "The house is a temple, he says; the king-sized bed in the master bedroom is a shrine. He sleeps on a folding cot. A devotee" (p. 191). The clumsy attempts of Judith, the Canadian social worker, whose mechanical and bookish knowledge take the place of sincere sympathy and understanding, as she admits her helplessness :

> We want to help, but our hands are tied in so many ways. We have to distribute money to some people, and there

> are legal documents — these things can be done. We have interpreters, but we don't always have the human touch, or may be the right human touch (p. 183).

This is contrasted with the suffering of bereaved Sikh family which cannot communicate in English. The old man who has lost his two sons in the crash requests Mrs. Bhave to tell the social worker 'God will provide, not Government' (p. 194).

Such situations pinpoint the cultural differences. The Canadians think that with money they can compensate for the losses of a father, a mother, a wife, a son, a daughter. They fail to understand the sentiments of ageing Sikh parents, as the social worker sarcastically comments :

> They think signing a paper is signing their son's death warrants, don't they? (p. 195).

Mrs. Bhave wants to say 'In our culture, it is a parent's duty to hope, but she can't say that because she knows they cannot understand her sentiments.' The story ends with Mrs. Bhave's statement :

> I do not know where this voyage I have begun will end.
> I do not know which direction I will take (p. 197).

This uncertainty is the fate of these immigrants and tragedy is a common phenomenon in their life immensely accentuated by the bicultural tensions.

Thus, we see that *The Middleman and Other Studies* reveal a new world in our midst, a world created by the transformation of the United States by new faces from all over the world, from 'nothing places' as Bharati Mukherjee puts it. They portray the immigrants in all their richness and variety reflected in American eyes, equally varied with fear, low suspicion or pure astonishment. The collection is about the straddling of two cultures, straining hard to reach a point of convergence. Bharati Mukherjee refers to this phenomenon in more explicit terms :

> It was not right to describe the American experience as one of the melting pot but a more appropriate word would be 'fusion' because immigrants in America did not melt into or were forged into something like their

> white counterpart but immigration was a two-way process and both the whites and immigrants were growing into a third thing by this interchange and experience.[22]

The fictional writings of Bharati Mukherjee comprising *Darkness* and *The Middleman* composed in the phase of Transition centre in the gripping dilemma of the protagonists who relentlessly try to overcome the native nostalgia. Quite a few of these characters behave and conduct themselves like immigrants much to the embarrassment of those who are in the process of acculturation. The story "Jasmine" in *The Middleman* anticipates Mukherjee's best known work *Jasmine* to be taken up in the next chapter.

REFERENCES

1. Bharati Mukherjee. *Darkness* (Toronto : Penguin Books, 1985, Indian reprint, 1990), p. 2.
2. Christine Gomez. "From Expatriation to Immigration : The Quest of Bharati Mukherjee with Special Reference to *Darkness*," in K.S. Ramamurti, ed. *Canadian Literature and Society* (Delhi : Pencraft International, 1996), p.136.
3. C.L. Chua. "Passage from India : Migrating to America in the Fiction of V.S. Naipaul and Bharati Mukherjee" in Emmanuel S. Nelson, ed. *Reworlding — The Literature of the Indian Diaspora* (New York : Greenwood Press, 1992), p. 56.
4. Mitali R. Pati. "Love and the Indian Immigrant in Bharati Mukherjee's Short Fiction," in Emmanuel S. Nelson, ed. *Bharati Mukherjee : Critical Perspectives* (New York : Garland Publishing, 1993), p. 197.
5. *Ibid.*, p. 206.
6. *Ibid.*, p. 198.
7. *Ibid.*, p. 203.
8. Sudha Pandya. "Bharati Mukherjee's *Darkness* : Exploring the Hyphenated Identity." *Quill*, Dec. 1990, p. 68.
9. Peter Nazareth, "Total Vision," *Canadian Literature* (Fall 1986), 184.
10. Carol, Sicherman. "Transport Me ... into the Hearts of Men" : Bharati Mukherjee's *Darkness*," *Kunapipi*, 14, 3, 1992, 83.
11. Christine Gomez. "From Expatriation to Immigration : The Quest of Bharati Mukherjee with Special Reference to *Darkness*," in K.S. Ramamurti, ed. *Canadian Literature and Society*, *op. cit*, pp. 139-40.
12. Alison B. Carb. "An Interview with Bharati Mukherjee," *The Massachusetts Review*, Winter 1988-89, 648.

13. Raban Jonathan. "Savage Boulevards, Easy Streets," *The New York Times*, 19 June 1988, p. 21.
14. John Coates. 'Bharati Mukherjee,' *Chicago Tribune*, 17 July 1989.
15. S. Mazumdar. "The Hollow Men and Women," *Financial Express*, 6 May 1990, 10.
16. Polly Shulman. "Home Truths," in *VLS* 66 (June 1988), 19.
17. Bharati Mukherjee. *The Middleman and Other Stories* (London : Virago Press, 1989), p. 3
18. Sibyl Steinberg. "Bharati Mukherjee," *Publisher's Weekly*, 25 Aug. 1989, p. 46.
19. Alison B. Carb. "An Interview with Bharati Mukherjee," *The Massachusetts Review*, Winter 1988-89, 648.
20. *Ibid*, pp. 653-54.
21. *Ibid*, p. 654.
22. Bharati Mukherjee, *The Hindustan Times*, 9 Feb. 1990, p. 3.

5

The Phase of Immigration

Bharati Mukherjee's later novels — *Jasmine* (1989), *The Holder of the World* (1993) and *Leave It to Me* (1997) — comprise her last creative phase conveniently termed here as the Phase of Immigration. By now she has travelled a long distance in terms of thematic perception and character portrayal. Beginning with an expatriate's uprooted identity in the early 70's, her creative faculty explored the transitional dilemma of characters in early 80's, whose acculturation bids were occasionally thwarted by the complexity of cultural plurality in the adopted land. However, after the publication of *The Middleman* (1988), the process of cultural acclimatisation appears to be complete and the characters betray the confidence of an immigrant, almost a naturalised citizen, in facing the challenges of human life.

In *Jasmine* (1989), Mukherjee tries to unravel the complicated layers of cross-cultural reality through a series of adventures which the heroine undertakes during her odyssey from Punjab to California via Florida, New York and Iowa. Her struggle symbolises the restless quest of a rootless person piqued by a depressing sense of isolation all around. The story opens with the village astrologer under his banyan tree foretelling Jasmine's 'widowhood and exile.' It all turns out just as nastily as he says it will, but at the same time Jasmine is a survivor, a fighter and adapter. Her journey through life leads Jasmine through many transformations — Jyoti, Jasmine, Jase and Jane via divergent geographical locales like Punjab, Florida, New York, Iowa and finally California. At every step Jasmine revolts against her fate and the path drawn for her. The narrative shuttles between past and present, between India of the narrator's early life and America of her present one. The past is Jyoti's childhood in the small village of Hasnapur, Punjab, her marriage to Prakash Vijh and the consequences leading to her departure to America. The present is her life as Jane in Baden, Iowa where she is a live-in-companion to Bud Ripplemeyer, a small town banker.

Jasmine's transformation from Jyoti to Jane had its own scars and stresses. Jyoti is born in a feudal village of Punjab, eighteen years after the partition riots. The fifth daughter and seventh of nine children of her parents, she is a dowryless, undesirable female child, a curse for them. However, she is bold and intelligent, the first ever likely student of Masterji fit for English education. She is a non-conformist, a rebel who questions the prophecies of the astrologer about her "widowhood and exile" in the harshest terms :

> "You're a cracy old man. You don't know what my future holds![1]

This irritates the fortune-teller and he chucks hard on her head and she falls on the ground getting a star-shaped scar on her forehead. This scar is seen as a curse to her but she treats it as her "third eye" and feels like becoming "a sage" (p. 5). She does not believe in the prevalent conviction that "Village girls are like cattle; whichever way you lead them, that is the way they will go" (p. 46). To exhibit the force of her belief she refuses to marry the widower selected by her grandmother and eventually ends up marrying Prakash Vijh in a court of law.

The cursed and hapless village girl in Jyoti becomes Jasmine, a city woman, wife of a modern man Prakash who wishes her "to call him by his first name" (p. 77). This christening means much to her :

> He gave me a new name : Jasmine. He said : "You are small and sweet and heady, my Jasmine. You'll quicken the whole world with your perfume (p. 77).

After marriage she becomes a true wife in the Indian sense of the term identifying her husband's wishes with those of hers. Prakash's ardent wish is to secure admission in some obscure American Institute of technology. They start dreaming about their life in

America but as the ill-luck would have it, Prakash falls a prey to the Khalsa Lions, the rebels demanding a separate land of Khalistan for Sikhs, on the very eve of his departure rendering Jasmine heart-broken and alone. A born fighter as she is, she does not allow this heart-rending tragedy to deter her courage. She plans to visit the supposed institute where Prakash had to get admitted and to burn herself a "Sati" on the campus of that engineering school. Jasmine's decision leaves her family aghast and they wonder "a village girl, going alone to America without job, husband or papers?" (p. 97).

Jasmine leaves for America on forged papers knowing not what future holds in store for her. But she is aware of the fate of her likes. She muses :

> We are the outcastes and deportees, strange pilgrims visiting outlandish shrines, landing at the end of tarmacs, ferried in old army trucks where we are roughly handled and taken to roped-off corners of waiting rooms where surly, barely wakened customs guards await their bribe. We are dressed in shreds of national costumes, out of season, the witted plumage of intercontinental vagabondage. We ask only one thing : to be allowed to land; to pass through; to continue (p. 101).

Jasmine is estranged by the uncertainties of her life in an unknown country :

> What country? What continent? We pass through wars, through plagues. I am hungry for news, but the discarded papers are in characters or languages I can not read (p. 101).

However, she travels to the New World on a shrimper called 'The Gulf Shuttle'. Jasmine's first encounter with America is a kind of what Malashri Lal says, a "regeneration through violence."[2] The captain of the ship, an ugly fellow, Half-Face who "had lost an eye and ear and most of his cheek in a paddy field in Vietnam" (p. 104) takes her to a remote motel of Florida and makes before her indecent proposals. Jasmine requests him that she is a deplorable Hindu widow and her "mission (is) to bring my husband's suit to America" (p. 114), he laughs at her idea : "Getting your ass kicked half way around the world just to burn a suit. I never heard such a fool notion" (p. 114). He remorselessly rapes Jasmine and this outrage is too much for an Indian widow. He sleeps after promising more sexual excitement later in the night. Jasmine goes to bathroom and decides "to balance her defilement with my (her) death" (p. 117) but before she could do so she discovers that she wants to live. Instantly she realizes : "I could not let my personal dishonor disrupt my mission." She extends her tongue and slices it, blood oozing — a perfect vengeful image of Goddess Kali out to defy and destroy the 'devil' who has violated her chastity. She kills the demon and for some moment remains perturbed :

> No one to call to, no one to disturb us. Just me and the man who had raped me, the man I had murdered. The room looked like a slaughter house. Blood had congealed on my hands, my chin, my breasts ... I was in a room with a slain man, my body blooded. I was walking death, Death incarnate (p. 119).

Jasmine's killing of Half-Face is a kind of self-assertion. Her decision to kill herself first, is a decision of a woman who lives for her deceased husband but the woman who kills Half-Face is prompted by her will to live to continue her life. "In killing Half-Face," writes Samir Dayal, "she experiences an epistemic violence that is also a life-affirming transformation."[3] Pondering over the agonising as well as transforming effect of evil Jasmine says :

> For the first time in my life I understood what evil was about. It was about not being human.... It was a very simple, very clear perception, a moment of truth, the kind of understanding that I have heard comes at the moment of death (p. 116).

After this violent encounter with the ugly world, Jasmine starts afresh; sans money, sans idea about the surroundings — hungry and thirsty, broken both in body and mind. Incidentally she happens to meet Lillian Gordon, a kind Quaker lady who harbours her, pities her situation, calls her Jazzy and teaches her to talk, walk and dress like an American. She advises her : "let the past make you wary, by all means. But do not let it deform you" (p. 131). Lillian

Gordon is committed to help the illegal immigrants. Later on she encourages Jasmine to proceed to New York for a suitable job with an introductory letter to her daughter staying there. After reaching New York Jasmine decides to visit her husband's former teacher Devinder Vadhera who has been instrumental in her husband's admission. His home in Flushing, Queens, is part of a Punjabi immigrant ghetto. Vadheras never try to come out of their four walls, the "artificially maintained Indianness" (p. 145). Jasmine remembers her five months sojourn at Flushing with pain and despair : "Flushing, with all its immigrant services at hand, frightened me" (p. 145). Again she recalls :

> Flushing was a neighborhood in Jullundhar. I was spiraling into depression behind the fortress of Punjabincss .... An imaginery brick wall topped with barbed wire cut me off from the past and kept me from breaking into future. I was a prisoner doing unreal time (p. 148).

Here among the Vadheras she is a helpless widow not entitled to enjoy life. This life is terrifying to her, "I wanted to distance myself from everything Indian, everything Jyoti-like" (p. 145). America has so many surprises for Jasmine in its "Pandora box." To her dismay she comes to know that Devinder Vadhera far from being a real Professor is a sorter of human hair. This fact unfolds, for the first time, the reality of immigrant life to her and she rationalises Vadhera's act :

> He needed to work here, but he did not have to like it. He had sealed his heart when he'd left home. His real life was in an unlivable land across oceans. He was a ghost, hanging on (p. 153).

This comprehension of reality is further confirmed by the taxi-driver who is a doctor from Kabul and confides to her, "we have to be here living like dogs" (p. 140).

In New York streets Jasmine sees "more greed, more people" (p. 140) like herself. New York seems to be "an archipelago of ghettos seething with aliens" (p. 140). Her failure in understanding the intentions of the American beggar is symbolic of confusion that grips an immigrant in an alien land. The American beggar abuses her and calls her a "foreign bitch." Jasmine, like the true immigrants is tossed between a desire for remembering her past and an equally pressing urgency to forget it :

> I feel at times like a stone hurtling through diaphanous mist, unable to grab hold, unable to slow myself, yet unwilling to abandon the ride I'm on. Down and down I go, where I'll stop, God only knows (p. 139).

The freedom loving spirit of Jasmine finds it difficult to cope with the conservative India represented by the Vadheras and after spending five frustrating months at Flushing one day, she deserts the Vadheras and sets forth for another adventure.

Next we see Jasmine in an apartment on Claremont Avenue, Manhattan with Taylor and Wylie Hayes as a caregiver to their adopted daughter, Duff. This is the best period of her stay in the States. She discovers to her excitement that Taylor is a true professor and at once feels impressed by his humane conduct :

> I fell in love with what he represented to me, a professor who served biscuits to a servant, smiled at her, and admitted her to the broad democracy of his joking (p. 167).

Taylor gives her a new name "Jase" and she is all excited about her life with the Hayeses. She recalls : "Duff was my child; Taylor and Wylie were my parents, my teachers, my family" (p. 165).

In the new surroundings marked by personal warmth, Jasmine becomes more Americanized, more confident of her proficiency in English but her instinctive Indian values do surface now and then. For instance, when she comes to know that Duff is not a natural child but an adopted one, her reactions are culturally revealing :

> I could not imagine a non-genetic child. A child that was not my own, or my husband's, struck me as a monstrous idea. Adoption was as foreign to me as the idea of widow remarriage (p. 170).

Her Indian sense of values cannot tolerate the sight of "naked bodies combing their hair in front of dresser mirrors" (p. 171). She records her disgust :

> Truly there was no concept of shame in this society.

> I'd die before a Sob Sister asked me about Half-Face (p. 171).

She again feels outwitted at Wylie's decision to leave Taylor for economist Stuart in search of "real happiness" (p. 181). She feels defeated :

> America had thrown me again. There was no word I could learn, no one I could consult, to understand, what Wylie was saying or why she had done it (pp. 181-82).

This is beyond imagination for Jasmine to think of snapping her bonds with her husband. She comes to realise the "liquidity" and "transitoriness" of human relationships in America. She gets the bitterest lesson :

> In America, nothing lasts. I can say that now and it doesn't shock me but I think it was the hardest lesson of all for me to learn. We arrive so eager to learn, to adjust, to participate, only to find the monuments are plastic, agreements are annulled. Nothing is forever, nothing is so terrible, or so wonderful, that it won't disintegrate (p. 181).

However, she is not unmindful of the positive side of American ethos. She appreciates the Americans for their democracy of thought and their sense of respect even for those doing menial works. The Western civilization has a "Work-Culture" and in this set up everybody is discharging his duty without any complex. She compares her own situation with the Mazbi woman who worked in her house at Hasnapur :

> In Hasnapur the Mazbi woman who'd stoked our hearth or spread our flaking, dried-out adobe walls with watered cow dung had been a maidservant. Wylie made me feel her younger sister. I was family, I was professional (p. 175).

Jasmine has experienced the best moments of stay in America in the company of Taylor and Duff who are like family for her. Taylor also starts loving her and she too wishes that her role as a "day-mummy" should never end. She is absorbed in the American world forgetting all about her strange mission as she herself accepts :

> Jyoti was now a sati-goddess; she had burned herself in a trash-cum-funeral pyre behind a boarded-up motel in Florida. Jasmine lived for future, for Vijh & Wife. Jase went to movies and lived for today (p. 176).

She thinks that she has got an established home and now she will no longer be haunted by rootlessness, "I had landed and was getting rooted" (p. 179) but still her destination is not reached and she is forced to run from New York. She sights the assassin of her husband, Sukhwinder, and runs for life to Iowa. But her escape is not a sign of her cowardice, it is 'life-affirming, "She (Jasmine) is running away for life not escaping from life which is a positive step."[4] Pushpa N. Parekh thinks that Jasmine's stay at Taylor's for two years is the most fruitful period of her life in America :

> This period in Jasmine's life is the most restful and comforting, emotionally and psychologically, intellectually, however, it is a phase of minute observations of complex inner deliberations on, and keen involvement in her new environment.[5]

Again her observations on Taylor-Wylie episode are very minute :

> Wylie's apparent "reasonless" abandoning of Taylor and Duff is a jolt back to the inexplicable and unexplainable nature of human action. Instead of fate or destiny or an unknown power being responsible for a family's break-up, Jasmine witnesses an American woman, Wylie, deliberately choosing to leave. Jasmine's inner monologues and silent reflections capture her deliberations on cultural differences and an immigrant woman's emotional adherence to her traditional beliefs while intellectually exploring the new avenues opened to her by the modern value systems.[6]

Jasmine's life in Iowa again begins with her chance meeting with Mother Ripplemayer, the Iowan counterpart of Lillian Gordon. She helps her getting a job in her son Bud's bank as a teller girl and after six months she is the live-in companion of Bud Ripplemayer. It seems that Bharati Mukherjee uses fate and chance as a 'problem-solving-device.' In her use of this device there is something like a "fairytale." Bud not only gives her a new life but also a new name — Jane. When Jane meets Bud he is "a tall, fit, fifty-year-old banker, husband of Karin, father of Buddy and Vern" (p. 14) but after six months he is a divorcee living with an illegal immigrant :

> Asia had transformed him, made him reckless and emotional. He wanted to make-up for fifty years of "selfishness", as he calls it (p. 14).

After one year he is a crippled man living with his Asian wife and adopted son, Du who is a Vietnamese brought from a refugee camp by him. Nobody is safe in violence torn America. Bud falls a victim to one Harlan Kroener who shoots him leaving maimed.

Jane likes Iowa because it is very much like Hasnapur. The farmers here are very much like the farmers of her own village "modest people, never boastful, tactful and courtly in their way" (p. 11). Bud is always uneasy with her past and never enquires of it. To quote Jane :

> My genuine foreignness frightens him. I don't hold that against him. It frightens me too (p. 26).

It is her strangeness that adds to her beauty :

> Bud courts me because I am alien. I am darkness, mystery, inscrutability. The East plugs me into instant vitality and wisdom. I rejuvenate him simply by being who I am (p. 200).

Jasmine's every movement is a calculated step into her Americanization and with each development a vital change is marked in her personality. Jasmine's flight to Iowa and her renaming as Jane is indicative of a slow but steady immersion into the mainstream American culture. Here we encounter a changed Jasmine — one who had murdered Half-Face for violating her chastity, now not only willingly embraces the company of an American without marriage but also is carrying his child in her womb. We are simply surprised at her act since every idea revolts at this form of an Indian widow. But one should never forget that she is a rebel who revolts at every step against the path drawn for her. She is an adapter, a survivor. Du is also a fighter who has survived eating worms and rodents in the refugee camp. Jasmine easily identifies herself with Du because both have made odysseous exploits in order to live. They "communicate silently in a no-questions asked relationship of strong identification : they come from the same "Third World" and share a common legacy of suffering and survival."[7]

An immigrant's life is in fact a series of reincarnations. He lives through several lives in a single life-time. This truth explains the condition of Bharati Mukherjee as well as that of Jasmine. As Mukherjee confides in one of her interviews :

> I have been murdered and reborn at least three times, the very correct young woman I was trained to be, and was very happy being, is very different from the politicized, shrill, civil rights activist I was in Canada, and from the urgent writer that I have become in the last few years in the United States.[8]

This statement has a marked similarity with Jasmine's outcry :

> There are no harmless, compassionate ways to remake oneself. We murder who we were so we can rebirth ourselves — in the images of dreams (p. 29).

Mukherjee, by subjecting her heroine to multiple codes of society and geographical locales seems to send the message that if one has to assimilate oneself to the mainstream culture of the adopted land, one should forgot one's past. This notion finds ample support from Jasmine's statement :

> Once we start letting go — let go just one thing, like not wearing our normal clothes, or a turban or not wearing a tika on the forehead — the rest goes on its own down a sinkhole (p. 29).

But this assimilation of Jasmine is not so smooth as it might appear on the surface :

> Fear, anger, pain, bitterness, confusion, silence, irony, humor, as well as pathos — underline her observations as she discovers for herself the undefined median between the preservation of the old world and the assimilation into the new one.[9]

All is well with Jane in Iowa till Du leaves for Los Angeles to join his sister. She has started identifying herself with Du because he is an immigrant like herself. Both are in a great hurry to become American, to forget the nightmares of their early lives. But Du's sudden departure shatters her world she has been so delicately nursing. Her passionate cry bursts out :

> How dare he leave me alone out here. How dare he retreat with my admiration, my pride, my total involvement in everything he did. His education was my education (p. 223).

Jasmine knows that "blood is thick" but the very "prospect of losing him (Du) is like a miscarriage" (p. 221). He has been a silent companion of Jasmine/Jane in all her bright and gloomy moments. Jasmine tries "to think like Lillian Gordon" at the moment who had put her on the Bus without showing any kind of grief, she orders herself "Don't cry, don't feel sorry for yourself" (p. 224) but this does not prove helpful. This sense of bereavement acquires intensity by the suicide of neighbouring Lutz boy Darrel who has been in love with her though she never responds to his love. The accumulated effect of these incidents and at this moment a call from Jasmine's former lover Taylor sets the path ready for her last adventure. Though "Bud's face, gray, ghostly, bodyless, floats in narrowing circles" (p. 239) around her she does not care for this man "who is losing his world" (p. 239). Already she has stopped thinking about Bud and at this moment Taylor and Duff come to take her to California where the new world, the promise of America is eagerly awaiting her. In deserting Bud and choosing Taylor Jasmine does not exchange between men but she changes her whole world. As she herself confides,

> "I am not choosing between men. I am caught between the promise of America and old-world dutifulness" (p. 240).

All through her stay for more than three years in Iowa Jasmine has been faithful to Bud. She has acted like an Indian wife who exults in her loyalty towards her husband. She has identified all her dreams and wishes with Bud's. She has sacrified all her individuality at the holy shrine of matrimony. She thinks that even the memory of the past life amounts to a kind of disloyalty to Bud because he feels frightened by her stories of Hasnapur. At Iowa she is a perfect wife who tries to please her husband by all means. She plays the temptress at his behest and hangs up all decency to yield to the sexual passion of a crippled person. Here she is very much like Indian women, bound to the "old world dutifulness" but the woman who walks out at last with Taylor "greedy with wants and reckless from hope" (p. 241) is positively an entirely different woman. This is a woman who is ready to see ahead, to ingratiate the best that future holds in store for her. She has no moral scruples and never feels guilty of her decision :

> It is not guilt that I feel, its relief .... Adventure risk, transformation : the frontier is pushing indoors through uncaulked windows.

She challenges the mocking astrologer who had declared her star-crossed :

> Watch me reposition the stars, I whisper to the astrologer who floats cross-legged above my kitchen stove (p. 240).

T. Padma[10] sees Jasmine's linking with Taylor "as a validation of her avowed belief — "Treat every second of your existence as a possible assignment from God" (p. 61) — a reaffirmation of the courage she mustered in killing the mad dog saying "I was not ready to die" (p. 56). From Jyoti to Jasmine, Kali to Jazzy and Jase to Jane is a long and arduous journey "hurtled through time tunnels" (p. 240), surviving the worst in life. From the special and unique nature of her evolving "Jasmine" self, Jane becomes, as her name implies, a non-entity, even a conscienceless "gold digger" in Karin's words (p. 195). From the "Sati-goddess" Jyoti (p. 176) to the Kali-Jasmine to "adventurous Jase" (p. 186) to "Plain Jane" (p. 26) has been an eventful, uneven odyssey; the protagonist's name changes as well as her shifts in places of residence become metaphors for an immigrant woman's 'process of uprooting and rerooting.'

Jane is expected to eventually become Bud Ripplemeyer's wife and the mother of their expected child. She, however, is a complex blend of the "silent woman," "the speaking person" and the "teller of tales." As the "silent woman" she accepts the almost preplanned and tailor-made itinerary of a certain predictable way of life with Bud. But her increasing sense of isolation and loss of self in this suffocating world is heightened by her inability to share with him her memories or reflections of the past, which are as much a part of her identity as the present. Bud prefers not to discuss her painful past. This is in sharp contrast to Taylor's disposition — "Taylor didn't want to change me. He didn't want to scour and sanitize the foreignness. My being different from Wylie or Kate didn't scare him" (p. 185).

Ready to sacrifice her own happiness and dreams, Jane almost acquiesces to become Bud's wife. It is through Du, their adopted Vietnamese son, that she wishes to sustain her identity as an "immigrant." All the forces in Iowa would eventually freeze her to conformity or continual alienation. Bud is uncomfortable with her tales of Hasnapur. He wishes her silent while Du, driven to quickly become thoroughly American, only cursorily pays heed to her stories about her Indian life. She realizes she cannot remake herself through Du "my transformation has been genetic; Du's was hyphenated," (p. 222). In evaluating her past and present and envisaging her future, she confronts the complexity and multiplicity of her identity as an immigrant woman.

Appearing self-possessed and patient, Jane, as we discover her through her interior monologues, is seething. Likening herself to a "tornado" she wonders over the changes that are yet to reshape her destiny :

> I still think of myself as caregiver, recipe giver, preserver. I can honestly say all I wanted was to serve, be allowed to join, but I have created confusion and destruction wherever I go. As Karin says, I am a tornado. I hit the trailer parks first, the prefabs, the weakest links. How many more shapes are in me, how many more selves, how many more husband? (p. 215).

In "telling her tale," the Jane and Jasmine selves of the protagonist seek to blend their "wants" and "dreams" into possibilities and realities. The range and the texture of the narrative voice reiterate the immigrant woman's personal journey as a new questing pioneer's movement from self-denial to self-realization.

Jasmine's restless move from one place to another betrays her gripping alienation and bewilderment. On more than one occasions she realises that she is an "outsider" and "other" in America — an illegal immigrant without passport, living among aliens whose ways she knows nothing about. She is always apprehensive about American being and thinking, suffers humiliation and disappointment. As she mutters : "This country has so many ways of humiliating, of disappointing" (p. 29). Again her failure to understand Wylie's decision to leave Taylor testifies to the fact that she is a poor immigrant. She comes from the third world where experiences are always painful and it is in sharp contrast to her experience of America. As she says : "For them, experience leads to knowledge, or else it is wasted. For me (or likes), experience must be forgotten, or else it will kill" (p. 33). She dresses like an American, puts on an American name but she can trust only Asians : "I trust only Asian doctors, Asian professionals. What we've gone through must count for something" (p. 32). She is loved by all for her Indianness which has made her a lovable and caring wife, an affectionate mother. She echoes her sentiment again and again :

> A good Hasnapur wife doesn't eat just because she is hungry. Food is a way of granting or withholding love (p. 216).
>
> ... ...
>
> I'll wait supper for you. Indian wives never eat before their husbands (p. 213).

The above statements show that even if she is living with an American in an American household, among American appliances her ideal is an Indian wife who is by nature self-sacrificing. Jane does not pay heed to Bud's entreaty to marry her because she thinks she is responsible "for Prakash's death, Bud's maiming." She is "a tornado, blowing through Baden" (p. 206). Jasmine never forgets her past which impinges upon her senses like the stench of the carcass of the dog she encounters early in her life. "She perpetually haunts, and is haunted by, her ghostly identities .... She shuttles between differing identities."[11]

Indeed, Jasmine is a rebel and revolutionary. She protests against rigours of Indian culture. Her protest, like that of Bharati Mukherjee herself, is not against Indian culture per se but against its relentiveness, its particular way of partially comprehending the world. She revolts against conservative Indian attitude towards poor widows who are treated like non-entities. She resents against the 'Sati' system which compels Indian women to sacrifice their life although they want to live. She rebukes the male dominating Indian society which discourages self-reliance in women. Her grudge is against the artificially maintained ghetto which bars the non-resident Indians from identifying themselves with the progressive ideals of the West. However, her native values determine substantially the quality of her life.

Bharati Mukherjee does not consider Jasmine "a good person," she is a "black-mailer" and a "murderer" who has dumped a good crippled man. But she considers her a "love goddess" a "life-force."[12] She is not moral in the conventional sense but her morality is her own way of looking at life. She is a 'path-finder' and pierces her way through the dense jungle of problems. Every movement adds to her self-confidence and her experience guides her future course of action. She is fluid and adjusting and justifies her each and every role. Mukherjee's following observations border on confessional note :

> The kinds of women I write about ... are those who are adaptable. We've all been raised to please, been trained to be adaptable as wives, and that adaptability is working to the women's advantage when we come over as immigrants.[13]

Outwardly Jasmine responds very promptly to the behavioural patterns of the American society and instantly inculcates it in her character. However, a tenacious Indianness seems to cling to the subsurface of her adaptations. Indira Bhatt pertinently comments :

> Jasmine takes a birdview of the American life and does not touch the deeper layers of values there.[14]

Had she been purely guided by the American values, she should have abandoned Bud at the time of his disability. She abandons Bud later on, no doubt, but this decision is a cumulative effect of the happenings — Du's departure, Darrel's suicide and Taylor's proposal :

> Even Jyoti to Jasmine, to Jase and Jane may appear to be real transformation of the personality of the protagonist;

> from Hasnapur to Jullundhar to Florida, Manhattan, Iowa may appear to be moving from old world values to the brave new world. But the person we see at the end of the novel moving away with Taylor, is very much the same person we encounter at the earlier stages in the novel.[15]

Sarah Curtis also subscribes to a similar view :

> By the end of the book she is almost all American, but quintessentially she is still Indian.[16]

In Jasmine's tug of war between 'old world dutifulness' and the 'progressive America,' a perceptive reader can unmistakably mark that the ongoing conflict hardly reaches a happy reconciliation. Ingenious attempts have been made by some scholars to trace autobiographical touches in Mukherjee's works and this is obviously a commonplace criticism on expatriate writers. Identifying Jasmine's predicament with that of her creator, Malashri Lal observes :

> A passport gives instant legal recognition, it does not determine instant cultural transfers. That truth explains Bharati Mukherjee's dilemma as also her Jasmine's restless moves.[17]

In attempting to resolve her crisis of identity through nomenclature — from Jyoti to Jasmine, to Jase and to Jane — coupled with changes in geographical contours — from Hasnanur to Jullundhar, to Florida, Manhattan, Iowa — Jasmine tries all external alternatives but to no avail. The person one sees at the end of the novel moving away with Taylor is very much the same one encounters at the earlier stages in the book. The movement without cannot necessarily mean transformation within in respect of one with the inherited Indian ethos.

Mukherjee explores other ramifications of cultural confrontation in *The Holder of the World.* (1993). It is also a tale about dislocation and transformation arising when two cultures come into contact with each other. This novel "has a wide canvas that sweeps across continents and centuries, cultures and religions. Immigration, exile, alienation and foreign lands have always been the colour of Mukherjee's palate and with *The Holder of the World*, she uses the familiar tones and shades to create a universe of infinite possibility and eternal time."[18] Here we witness an unlikely and intriguing meeting of two worlds, the Puritan 17th and early 18th century American world trying to come to terms with the Mughal view of Indian life. In a startling commingling of history and imagination, Mukherjee lights up the making and very nature of the American consciousness in this novel. The inspiration behind this "fantastic" story was an ordinary incident on an ordinary day. In an interview, Mukherjee recalled :

> The novel got started because I was at an auction of Sotheby in New York.... Whatever money my husband and I save is spent on Indian miniature painting and my aesthetics for the novel evolves out of my love for Indian miniature painting.[19]

It was here that she saw a miniature titled "A European Woman in Aurangzeb's Court". A Caucasian woman stood resplendent in full Moghul dress and Mukherjee "suddenly realized that I was looking at a woman who three hundred years back had taken a lot of risks, had transformed herself." Earlier it was always the journey from East to West and the accompanying Chamelion-like changes, but now this trip is in the opposite direction.

The novel generated favourable response from the critics all over the world and people acknowledged Mukherjee's skill in blending imaginary creations with historical facts. *The New York Times Book Review* admired *The Holder of the World* in the following terms :

> Ms Mukherjee draws us with vigour and scrupulous attention to detail across time — from the present to the 17th and early 18th centuries — and space — from Salem, Massachusetts to the Coast of Coromandel, in India — into the footsteps of not one but two extraordinary women... (an) extraordinary novel.... [20]

Uma Parameswaran has all praise for Mukherjee's concept of virtual reality. In a review of the novel she writes :

> In reconstructing a piece of Raj History, Mukherjee joins other novelists from her native India, such as Manohar Malgonkar (The Princes, The Devil's Wind), Kamala Markandaya (The Golden Honeycomb), and more recently, Gita Mehta (Raj). She adds another dimension

> to linear narrativization by using the concept of virtual reality....[21]

Such adulatory comments are not misplaced because *The Holder of the World* demonstrates a consummate artistry to blend fact and fiction head and heart, science and religion, East and West, history and imagination, the Old World and the New World. Mukherjee has dedicated this novel 'To Ann Middleton, and all travellers to utmost shores'. Here she creatively travels in time and space, past and present, exotic and known and this lends to this novel an extraordinary dimension never seen in her writings before. It is a quest for identity, transformation and translation of protagonist's personality under the stress of the circumstances.

The title *The Holder of the World*, the literal translation of Alamgir, is a name for the Mughal emperor, Aurangzeb. This is the story of two white women, one living in the seventeenth century and the other, in the present one, who becomes obsessed with retracing the former's transformation from a Puritan girl brought up at Salem in Massachusetts to the 'bibi' of a Hindu King. For a brief, lightning quick flash, two women face the brown-skinned Indian maidservant, Bhagmati. The artist creates a complex plot, communicating through the two main voices the dense landscape of her novel. It begins with Beigh (looks like 'Bee,' sounds like 'Bay-a') Masters, an assets researcher, a job she describes as "uniting people and possessions; it's like matching orphaned socks, through time" (p. 5). Beigh Masters is the narrator of the story. She makes the intentions and objectives of the author transparent in the very beginning of the novel :

> I live in three time zones simultaneously, and I don't mean Eastern, Central and Pacific. I mean the past, present and the future (p. 5).

At the moment, she is busy reading *Auctions and Acquisitions*, one of the trade magazines in her field with her lover Venn Iyer, an Indian Computer Scientist sitting beside her. She learns from the book that though people and their property get separated from one another, "Nothing is ever lost, but continents and centuries sometimes get in the way" (p. 5). It gives her a clue to a large gem acquired by a small museum situated between Salem and Marble head. Now she is trying to locate what her client calls the most perfect diamond in the world, 'The Emperor's Tear.' It belonged to the last of the great Mughal Kings, Aurangzeb, and was stolen from him during a battle against Raja Jadav Singh, the Hindu lover of the Seventeenth Century Puritan Woman Hannah Easton. As Beigh tries to trace the diamond she gets obsessed with Hannah's life more than the diamond itself :

> It isn't the gem that interests me. It's the inscription and the provenance. Anything having to do with Mughal India gets my attention. Anything about the Salem Bibi, precious-as-pearl feeds me (p. 5).

Beigh lives with her Indian lover for nearly three years. "He animates information. He's out there beyond virtual reality, re-creating the universe, one nanosecond, one minute at a time" (p. 5). Both Beigh Masters and her Indian lover are dealers in the things of past. They claim "The past presents itself to us" (p. 6). Venn is of the view that "Every time-traveler will create a different reality — just as we all do now. No two travelers will be able to retrieve the same reality ... History is a big saving bank" (p. 6).

The use of time travel to help Beigh (and the reader) unravel the mystery of 'The Emperor's Tear' is a clever ruse. Her searches around museums, East India Company documents and colonial literature, her travels to India and auctions all over the world, are commendable efforts to reconstruct a daring woman's odyssey. She makes it seem plausible that a seventeenth-century Puritan woman could have ventured into a different culture and met a Mughal ruler contemporary of the Sun King, of Peter the Great and of Oliver Cromwell. Beigh's painstaking piecing together of Hannah's life is like building a picture-puzzle across time. Solving the last clue through computer magic turns it into the stuff of high-tech occult. While it satisfies emotionally, one obviously remains unconvinced.

Arshia Sattar comments that Mukherjee "is at her most eloquent and intelligent when she explores the complexities of cultural confrontation and the politics of "otherness."[22] Here she presents the difference between the Old and the New Worlds, represented by America and India, as a clash of value systems, a confrontation between an austere, stark society and a culture in which nothing is more important than the celebration of beauty. As the narrator proceeds it unfolds the story of the Puritan woman of 17th century Hannah Easton, born in the American Colonies in 1670, "a person undreamed of in Puritan society" (p. 59). Inquisitive, vital, awake to her own sense of self and purpose, she is "a spiritual aristocrat in an age of common believers." "She is from a different time, the first person, let alone the first woman, to have had these thoughts, and this experience, to have been formed in this particular crucible" (p. 59).

As Beigh Masters fumbles for more details about Hannah Easton, she discovers in her a remote relative of hers. As she proudly claims "I'm part of this story, the Salem Bibi is part of the tissue of my life" (p. 21). She discovers that 'Rebecca Easton (Hannah's mother) nee Walker's grand mother was a cousin of Charles Jonathan Samuel Muster's father' (p. 21), with whom Beigh claims her kinship though she is not sure "Back on the scepter'd isle, three hundred years ago, we were Musters, Or Musterers" (p. 10). She presents a detailed description of the settlement and adventures of the Musters on the Ellis Island and their coming to terms with the Eastons :

> The first Masters to scorn the strained stability of his lot was one Charles Jonathan Samuel Muster, born in Morpeth, Northumberland. In 1632, a youth of seventeen, C.J.S. Muster stowed away to Salem in a ship heavy with cows, horses, goats, glass and iron. What extraordinary vision he must have had, to know so young that his future lay beyond the waters...at the mercy of heathen Indians and the popish French. By 1640 he was himself the proprietor of a three-hundred acre tract that he then leased to an in-law recently arrived, and then he returned to Salem and the life of a sea trade, Jamaica to Halifax. Curiosity or romance has compelled us to slash, burn, move on, ever since (pp. 10-11).

The year that young Charles Muster secreted himself among the livestock abroad the 'Gabriel,' a noble woman in India died in child birth. That noble woman was the wife of most lucretious Mughal King Shahjahan, Mumtaz Mahal, whose memory the king immortalized by erecting the Tai Mahal, a symbol of everlasting love. Three years later when Jonathan was barely twenty, 'he abandoned the country and built the first of many houses on a overlook commanding a view of the sea and the spreading rooftops of Salem. For the rest of his life he scuttled between civilized Salem and the buck skinned fringes of the known world, out beyond Worcester, then Springfield, then Barrington, gathering his tenant's tithes of corn and beans, salted meat and barrels of ale, selling what he couldn't consume and buying more tracts of uncleared forest with the profit.... He was a New World Emperor" (pp. 11-12).

Beigh visits the Museum of Maritime Trade and finds that 'the curator's note cards celebrate only Puritan pragmatism. There is no order, no hierarchy of intrinsic value or aesthetic worth; it's a fly's eye view of Puritan history" (p. 12). She also comes across the Mughal opulence 'flashy with decoration' (p. 12) and she wonders over the gulf between two worlds :

> What must these worlds have thought, colliding with each other? How mutually staggered they must have been; ... (p. 12).

The opulence of the Eastern World, their love for gold, diamond and jewellery drives the Westerners to disdain and despair. But their sense of snobbery does not permit them to kneel-down before the Eastern culture. They revel in their own sense of pride and superiority as is obvious from one of the inscriptions in the Museum which records their reactions :

> We beat those Asians because our pots are heavy and black and our pothooks contain no jewels. No paintings, no inlays of rubies and pearls. Our men wore animal skins or jerkins of crude muslin and our women's virtue was guarded by bonnets and capes and full skirts. Those Indian guys wore earrings and dresses and necklaces. When they ran out of space on their bodies they punched holes in their wives' noses to hang more gold and pearl chains. Then they bored holes in their wives' ears to show off more junk, they crammed gold bracelets all the way up to their elbows so their arms were too heavy to lift, and they slipped new rings on their toes and thumbs so they could barely walk or make a fist (pp. 12-13).

Beigh Masters hunts for every minute detail about Hannah and she knows 'traces of Salem Bibi pop up from time to time in inaccessible and improbable little museums like this one. They get auctioned and sold to anonymous buyers. I believe I know her identity, and the anonymous donor' (p. 14). She is an ardent researcher, full of vigour, bubbling with confidence and having faith in her sincerity to achieve her goal. She dilates on her personality and the mental make-up at this juncture :

> There is surely one moment in every life when hope surprises us like grace, and when love, or at least its promise, landscapes the jungle into Eden (p. 15).

She is confident of finding this Eden, passing through the jungle like obscure museums and auctions around the world. As she goes through the photographic records of Hannah's life in a museum in Massachusetts she gets the vision of the Old World, its exotic inhabitants etc. :

> In a maritime trade museum in Massachusetts, I am witnessing the old world's first vision of the New, of its natives, of its ferocious, improbable shapes, of its monstrous women, that only the Salem Bibi could have described or posed for (p. 16).

The largest painting bears a catalogue name *The Apocalypse*, but the narrator calls it '*The Unravish'd Bride.*' In this painting "beautiful Salem Bibi stands on the cannon-breached rampart of a Hindu fort" (p. 17). In another painting she notices "Salem Bibi's lover, once a sprightly guerrilla warrior, now slumps against a charred tree trunk. He grasps a nephrite jade dagger hilt carved in the shape of a ram's head and, with his last blood-clotted breath, pledges revenge" (p. 17). Salem Bibi becomes a co-wanderer of Beign Masters, a constant source of vital energy, inspiration, adventure, odyssey, always whispering in her ears 'to go' :

> Fly as long as hard as you can, my co-dreamer! Scout a fresh site on another hill. Found with me a city where lions lie with lambs, where pity quickens knowledge, where desire dissipates despair! (p. 19).

Now she has the confidence to claim that she knows Hannah's ins and outs : I know her like a doctor and a lawyer, like a mother and a daughter. With every new thing I've learned, I've come imperceptibly closer to the Emperor's Tear...

> Three hundred years ago, it existed in her hands; I know where she came from and where she went. I couldn't care less about the Emperor's Tear, by now. I care only about the Salem Bibi (p. 19).

With this claim of Beigh Masters sufficient ground of plausibility is prepared. Now, we are ready to plunge our head in the details of Hannah's extraordinary life. Though, her movement has been a circular one, by no means she remains the same Hannah on her return to Salem. India has transformed her sensibility with the resultant change in her personality.

Hannah Easton was the only surviving child of Edward and Rebecca Easton, nee Rebecca Walker of Brookfield, in the Massachusetts Bay Colony. First the Walkers had settled in Boston, or even Rhode Island but by 1653 Elias Walker, his wife and infant daughter, Rebecca, arrived in Brookfield and leased, from their distant relatives the Masters, three hundred acres of prime Quabaug River bluff and bottom land. At that time, Brookfield was a hesitant hilltop Puritan outpost deep inside Nipmuc country. Elias Walker held the usual attitudes of his time, and ours, toward the Indians : they are children, they are trusting; they are proud and generous. Even capable of nobility. But at heart they are savages : bestial, unspeakably cruel. Eight years later, the Walkers gained a neighbour, a sickly looking but resourceful recent arrival (from England) by the name of Edward Easton, who purchased with his English savings a brown ribbon of a field, a rickety shed, a cabin with privy and two barns. At the age of 15 in 1668, Rebecca Walker got married to Edward Easton. Hannah was born of this marriage after two years.

In Old World, Edward Easton had been an East India Company man with a sedentary occupation. Beigh searches for more details about Edward's life and gets plenty of clues to reconstruct his life. She goes through East India Company ledger books, letters, books and papers stored in the India Office in white hall. Edward Easton's entries stand out because of the singular primacy and angularity of his handwriting. Beigh, a twenty-year old girl, really contemplating her place in the universe and the ways of the World had appropriated an ancestor, a man who had gone before her, and though he was writing of strangers, she cherished his observations like an intimate letter from home :

> A petty ruler on the Coromandel Coast of India is given the gifts of armour, a wool coat and a spying glass.
>
> A ship on its way to Masulipatnam is stocked with 1420 hogs and 250 oxen (p. 23).

What is known about the life of Edward, Hannah's father, is that he headed for the outer rings of settlements stopping over first in Billerica, then in Chelmsford, then in Lancaster. He was offered a modest book keeping job by John White's son-in-law, the Reverened Joseph Rowlandson, Lancaster's first minister — then in Worcester, and finally either running out of energy or finding in Brookfield the dreamscape for starting over. Beigh is proud of her discovery and boasts :

> I was perhaps the only scholar in the world who had traced the work of an obscure clerk from London to Massachusetts. I could sense all the movements in his life, his determination to remake his life before it was too late, to go west to the colony instead of east, where surely his East India clerkship could have led him. I felt the same psychic bond with Edward Easton that Keats did with the revelers on the Grecian Urn (p. 25).

On September 29, 1671 Hannah turned a year old and first toddled far enough away by herself to be brought back by a Solicitous Nipmuc. On that very day Edward Easton died of a bee sting while savouring the poetic paradox in an imported, treasured copy of *Paradise Lost* and the physical paradox of constipation's painful pleasures in his outdoor privy. Hannah lost her mother Rebecca a twenty-two-year-old widow when the Nipmuc laid siege to Brookfield in the month of August in 1675. Rebecca loved to sing. The little daughter had a disturbing memory of her mother which haunted her wherever she went. Her mother had deserted her in a Brookfield forest to run away with her American-Indian lover. Hannah knew that "It is necessary not only to retain the memory of her beloved, absent mother, but to deny its final blinding, lustful image. To preserve above all the orphan's tragic tale above the wicked woman's demonic possession" (p. 30). Hannah, a Puritan child was overburdened. "She had witnessed the Fall, not Adam's Fall, Rebecca's Fall. Her mother's Fall infinitely more sinful than the Fall of a man" (p. 30). But one thing is without question that "Hannah Easton, whatever the name she carried in Massachusetts, in England, in India or even into history to this very day, loved her mother more profoundly than any daughter has ever loved a mother" (p. 30).

Mukherjee has quite skilfully brought together the 17th century Puritan American society with the more liberated present day American society. Here we see Beigh Masters, a modern American researcher claiming her affinity with Easton family, comparing the circumstances of her own life with that of Rebecca and Hannah Easton :

> Like Rebecca, I have a lover. One who would seem alien to my family. A lover scornful of our habits of self effacement and reasonableness, of our naive or desperate clinging to an imagined continuity. Venn was born in India and came over as a baby. His family are all successful; there was never question of anything different. He grew up in a world so secure I can't imagine it, where for us security is another kind of trap, something to be discarded as dramatically as Rebecca stepped out of dog-blooded widow's weeds into a life of sin and servitude (p. 31).

Hannah, 'the somber orphan' (p. 39) is brought to Salem by Robert and Susannah Fitch. They rear her up with love and affection. Hannah has an extraordinary skill for needle work and soon her reputation reaches the masses :

> Temptation dogged the sensuous Hannah everywhere : in rich clients' halls as she delivered her handiwork of velvet gowns and quilted underskirts, coats flirty with ladders of bowknots and lingerie under sleeves, and caps of sheerest white muslin; at the baker's as she passed by selves of German fried and sugared breads.... (p. 42).

Even at the age of twelve, Hannah Easton's work is known and families who would not have admitted her step-parents to their parlours insist on showing her inside, offering her cakes and tiny tokens of additional payment. Susannah, her stepmother, praises her needle work skill, but fears the wantonness of spirit it betrays. However, such is the fame of Hannah's work and such is the charm of her magical personality that soon a marriage proposal comes for her from the Pynchons, one of New England's upstanding families. But Robert Fitch politely refuses the offer. The narrator thinks that after all it was for her own good as well as for the good of the country because "if Solomon Pynchon's marital overture had been accepted, the history of the United States would have been profoundly altered" (p. 57).

Hannah marries Gabriel Legge, the same man who had been courting her intimate friend Hester Manning who was found one day dead, fully recognizing the fact that he is untrustworthy. May be she is unconsciously imitating her mother's behaviour — running off with a treacherous yet exotic alien. "He claimed to be the son of the owner of the *Swallow*, three hundred and twenty tons. He had come from London, but hailed from Ireland, to scout the colonies for investment, for new forms of imports and exports to the New World to mark its growing stature, its great wealth and taste for finer things" (p. 62). The tall and dashing Gabriel Legge has an eye patch. But there is no doubt that he has an extraordinary capacity for making stories : "Tortured? Punished? Heroic? No one knew for sure. He had a thousand stories of imprisonment by Turks; banishment to forests; brigands, highway men, pirates" (p. 63).

Hannah's acceptance of Gabriel Legge, a man of dubious character raises a lot of questions in the mind of the narrator and at last she comes to the conclusion that unconsciously she imitates her mother by this act :

> Why would a self-possessed, intelligent, desirable woman like Hannah Easton suddenly marry a man she recognized as inappropriate and untrustworthy? Why would she accept Hester Manning's castoff, or betrayer? Guilt, perhaps, a need to punish herself for the secret she was

> forced to carry? Unconscious imitation of her mother, a way of joining her by running off with a treacherous alien? Gabriel Legge with his tales of exotic adventure was as close to the Nipmuc lover as any man in Salem. She sought to neutralize her shame by emulating her mother's behaviour (p. 69).

Later on the narrator takes recourse to philosophy and rationalizes her act :

> We do things when it is our time to do them. They do not occur to us until it is time; they cannot be resisted, once their time has come. It's a question of time, not motive. (p. 70)

Hannah finds to her dismay that Gabriel's father far from being a shipowner is an indebted drunk from Morpeth. Gabriel's life too is a mystery. "He could describe the interior of a Mongol tent, the smell of camels, the pink flesh inside the trunk of a raja's elephant, but he could not, or would not, answer the simplest question about the ships he sailed or the captains he served" (p. 71).

However, Hannah is inquisitive and tries to drink every draught of the life's cup. When Gabriel goes to his mysterious missions she finds a good engagement in the duty of a nurse. She can now use the same needle efficiently to the skull of men which she once used on clothes. Gabriel Legge proposes her to accompany him to India where he works as a junior factor in East India Company. Such is the curiosity of Hannah that she instantly accepts the offer and sets for India leaving aside her fortune and reputation in Stepney, England. While in England Hannah's perceptive eyes are quite alert to notice the attitude of American colonies towards the English Crown. She notices mutually contradictory feelings in two groups of people. On the one hand there are colonists who are "not grateful or respectful enough to the Crown and the Mother Country; the colonists were ignorance personified and insufficiently ashamed of their backwardness" (p. 72). For them 'England was refined and cultured' and colonies were 'soiled and sinful' (p. 72). On the other hand, there are colonists who are 'proud of their backwardness... they revealed in using and broadening their own American accent, which had already ironed out the multifarious wrinkles of British regionalism" (p. 73).

Hannah's arrival in India in 1695 is set against a period of tumultuous political and economic activity. Here she, as well as, we the readers confront the surly realities of British industrialists in India. "They had not come to India in order to breed and colonize, or even to convert. They were here to plunder, to enrich themselves" (p. 99). But Hannah's primary concern in this new world appears to be 'to peel the superficiality and social grace and dwell beneath it in a quest for a meaningful life. In fact, as soon as she steps on the shores of the Coromandel Coast, she feels an instinctive sense of belonging and decides that she did not "aspire to return to England upon the completion of Gabriel's tour" (p. 104). Hannah knew "she'd been transported to the other side of the world, but the transportation was more than mere 'conveyancing', as it was for Gabriel and the others. Many years later she called the trip, and her long residence in India, her "translation" (p. 104). Hannah is alive to the life around her. She is not afraid of the 'exotica' instead she is thrilled. It is this curiosity and enthusiasm towards life which makes her a contemporary of the narrator who cannot withhold her sense of admiration :

> Of all the qualities I admire in Hannah Easton that make her entirely our contemporary in mood and sensibility, none is more touching to me than the sheer pleasure she took in the world's variety (p. 104).

She knows that she has come half-way round the globe and the life in the Indian sub-continent is entirely different. She cannot use her own western parametres for measuring this world. Her reactions are that of a tourist :

> She was, in some original sense of the word (as a linguist is to language), a tourist. She was alert to novelty, but her voyage was mental interior. Getting there was important, but savoring the comparison with London or Salem, and watching her life being transformed, that was the pleasure. She did not hold India up to inspection by the lamp of England, or of Christianity (p. 104).

Her scale of values has been fixed early in her life. The nightmarish vision of her mother's elopement always haunts her mind. So

> if she judged the world from a single, unassailable place, it might have been from a forest in Brookfield, before the expulsion from that New World Eden... She did not fear the unknown or the unexplored. Her character was shaped on romps with Rebecca in the woods around Brookfield. And she needed time to sort out her errands — oh, so many errands! — in this vast new jungle (pp. 104-105).

During their voyage her husband endlessly talked about the life and society in India. He had tried to explain her that every one on Coromandel, belonged to a caste, if he was Hindu, a right-hand or left-hand caste, and everyone was either Shia or Sunni if he was Muslim. They all spoke different languages, they owed fidelity to different masters, they worshipped different gods, and their ancestors had come from different countries. It was all nightmarish for her. The immense variety was thrilling and exciting but it had been inconceivable to a Puritan soul like Hannah's. Her world was not so varied, not so diverse. So she wondered that here are "not just pagans and Muhammadans, but different gods and different ways of worshipping the same God" (p. 100).

Right from the moment Hannah sets her feet on Indian soil she is aware of the fact that she belongs to the land and people of this country are her brethren, and that she has got nothing to do with the race of those Britishers who have come here to plunder, to lead a life of comfort, lechery and convenience. Her encounter with English women, the wives of other factors, furthers her impatience with their pretensions to nobility and their self-conscious superiority among the local community. These were women who led ordinary lives in England but claimed command and respect here, always eager to display it in all its vulgarity. Martha Ruxton and Sarah Higginbotham are both examples of English snobbery and disdain characteristic of the women in the colonies. Their life of reason and etiquette is sharply opposed to the dubiously adventurous and morally ambivalent lives of their husbands whose 'bibis' become the primary topic of conversation among these women :

> Any servant with a new sari, any cheekiness detected, anything missing, meant a good serving girl had passed over to bibihood. Bibis were simultaneously beneath notice, no more than cute little pets like monkeys or

> birds, and devious temptresses, priestesses of some ancient, irresistible and overpowering sensuality (p. 131).

Hannah senses this obsession with bibis early during her stay in Fort St. Sebastian : "It seemed to Hannah that bibis, suspected and real, were at the center of female conversation in white town" (p. 131). The bibis are characterized by their sheer fleetingness and inability to tie down the English man for a lasting commitment. From the women's point of view, the bibi was an object to be at once ignored and overlooked but also to be suspiciously avoided. The bibi, Hannah is told, has to be admitted as a natural consequence of married life for "accommodation was synonymous with expatriate femininity" (p. 134). Hannah's bemused reception of this ordained truth testifies to her open-mindedness and capacity to view a situation from a perspective other than that of conventional society. She treated her situation as much redeemed :

> Hannah felt herself exempt from the bibi jealousies of a Sarah or Martha.... She had not led the desperate sort of life, like Sarah, that substituted gratitude for tolerance. She was a faithful wife who had attracted her share of suitable beaux and suitors, and who resisted courtings and temptations even when expectations and opportunities presented themselves (pp. 43-44).

For the freedom loving spirit of Hannah India is an ideal place. The narrator contrasts the house in Fort St. Sebastian with her former houses she lived in :

> In Brookfield, in Stepney and Salem, a house was a barricade to stop encroachment. Outdoors was the prowling ground for Satan and his companions; indoors was furnished, tamed and therefore safe. But the house that she was to live in, like all houses in Fort St. Sebastian, was built to entice crystal-bright tropical starlight, spume-slented breeze, bugs, birds and butterflies through its huge barred windows. There were terraces shiny as marble, balconies made of hardy woods, a flat roof for evening walks — ground level at night being considered unsafe — and turreted parapets. Behind the main house were the gardens, kitchen sheds, servants' shed and stables (pp. 118-19).

This description at once gives us a clue to the life of luxury and comfort led by the East India Company men during the Mughal period. To Shakuntala Bharvani, "It is very much a colonial novel at one level, with several details of colonial life woven in."[23]

While fusing history with fiction, Mukherjee never shirks from reflecting post-colonial anxiety. The lucretious life style, cruelty, lechery, the Britishers' feeling of disdain towards the natives are contradicted with the deplorable plight of the Indian masses. "The fort in which the Britishers lived was Little England. The Fort St. George Council's penal code encouraged straight and narrow living. Uncleanness, lying, cheating, drunkenness, swearing, missing morning or evening prayers, using seditious words, mutinying, dueling, all were punishable with whippings, mountings of the "wooden horse," confinement and fines. When caught. When admitted (pp. 127-28). The factors believe that their life in India is extraordinary and they are the very angels sent by the British God, the British Crown. They feel that they have a licence to commit whatever atrocities they like in view of their 'White superiority.' "Self-pity, unaccountability and hypocrisy were recast as virtues and renamed forgiveness, solidarity and tolerance" (p. 128). The novel also focusses our attention on the mysterious deaths of these factors who were more or less victims of intrigue planned by their own counterparts. The Chief Factor Cephus Prynne's body was recovered in deplorable condition. However, Hannah "looked on Cephus Prynne's murder as emancipation... the workings of an alien providence" (p. 163).

Hannah has an altogether different experience with the first manifestation of a bibi that she comes across in the form of Bhagmati. Pulling herself down from the terrace of Hannah's house, she is dressed in sheer muslin white which mesmerizes Hannah's consciousness. It is an image that persists in her mind as suggestive of the sensuality, magical attraction and passionate representation of this land. In fact, as Gabriel Legge sets out with the Marquis on a mission of piracy, Hannah feels no remorse or longing for her old world, for she has yet to come to terms with this passion, with the sensuality and life of emotion which Bhagmati represented in that fleeting moment on the terrace :

> She was not ready to entomb herself in Morpeth or London. She didn't feel bereft — of roots, of traditions — as Martha and Sarah professed to feel. Instead she felt unfinished, unformed (p. 163).

Now "Hannah felt herself no more at home in England than she did in the Coromandel. She was deficient in that genetic impulse toward teary-eyed patriotism" (p. 164).

With Gabriel Legge turning to piracy and becoming 'the Robinhood of the Coromandel Coast' (p. 167) she is not left with much option. Circumstances of her life start changing at a frantic pace in the year 1700. First she leaves Gabriel on grounds of faithlessness and next sees his ship sinking. She herself should have been drowned when a bridge collapsed but she is saved by Jadav Singh, the Raja of Devgad only to become his bibi afterwards. Is it not ironical that the same Hannah who leaves her husband for keeping a 'bibi' in the end becomes a 'bibi' herself carrying an illegitimate child? However, this incident is imperative for the total transformation of her personality, because her yearning for a kind of passionate salvation as a way of recreating her mother's choice in the forest is largely fulfilled in her encounter with Raja Jadav Singh. "Her courtship with the Raja indicates a relationship based entirely on Indian, 'Eastern' values and morality with little reference to the life left behind."[24] He offers Hannah a life of limitless possibilities and sensuous pleasures undreamed of in the English world. It is this experience of being overwhelmed in love, of being possessed to the point of distraction that Hannah embraces with the totality of her being and little moral speculation. "In Massachusetts Bay, life had been so hard, the summer so short, that the freaks of nature were given less opportunity to emerge and no comfort to thrive" (p. 173). But India opens new avenues of life for her. She is now ready to embrace like her mother 'Ravana', her alien lover. She identifies herself completely with her Indian lover. She has seen 'Firangis' plundering the Indians but what mesmerizes her is not the profit-hungry motives of 'firangis' but "the sturdiness of a religious faith that allowed hundreds of thousands of devotees to worship a god-head that chose to reveal itself as a scarlet-faced, yellow-furred, long-tailed monkey" (p. 170). She is very afraid before coming into actual contact with Raja Jadav Singh. She cannot hide her scepticism towards the Eastern faith :

> The idea of Hinduism was vaguely frightening and even more vaguely alluring to Hannah. English attitudes saw Islam as a shallow kind of sophistication; Hinduism a profound form of primitivism ... Muslims had restrictions, which were noble and manly; Hindus had taboos, which were superstitious and cowardly. Hindus were unreasonable, and unreachable, so tradition-bound that their minds were considered undeveloped, except for a wily ruthlessness among the trading castes (p. 219).

She had "a Christian's skepticism about other faiths, bolstered by a Muslimized intolerance for idolatry" (p. 220). On entering the new world, the world of Hindus she discovers in herself an urge 'to be able to name and memorize the new' (p. 225). She wants to embrace this world only to sacrifice herself at the altar of true love :

> She wanted the Raja and nothing else, she would sacrifice anything for his touch and the love they made. What she felt for the Raja was of a different order from what she had felt for Gabriel, or not dared to feel for Hubert. Gabriel and Hubert, for all their distinctive eccentricities, were men cast in one familiar mold, men who thrilled and disappointed within a predictable range. The Raja was an agent of Providence. He had saved her life, then saved her from the chilly, unfulfilled life of a governess (pp. 229-30).

Jadav Singh continues to court her one quarter of each night for a fortnight. This alters the sensibility of Hannah. The Eastern love makes her more emotional. She is aware of the transformation of her mentality, her whole personality :

> With Gabriel she had clung to Salem's do's and don'ts. She had pulled and pummeled the familiar rules, hoping they'd help make sense of her own evolution. With Jadav Singh, she'd finally accepted how inappropriate it was in India — how fatal — to cling, as White Towns tenaciously did, to Europe's rules. She was no longer the

> woman she'd been in Salem or London. The 'qasbas' and villages of Roopconda bore no resemblance to the fading, phantom landscapes where she'd lived in old and New England. Everything was in flux on the Coromandel Coastline (p. 234).

Ultimately Hannah discovers that "the survivor is the one who improvises, not follows, the rules" (p. 234). This comes as an indirect message of the author herself. She stresses now and again in almost all her fictional writings that only those people can survive in an alien world who are elastic and who can shape themselves according to the availability of space by improvising upon their native rules.

Jadav Singh's death and Hannah's encounter with Emperor Aurangzeb mature her experiences in terms of her journey to the world of the mysterious East. She is ready to protect her Indian lover inspite of his dissociation from her. The suspension of morality and the openness to new experiences make Hannah confront Aurangzeb and even bow to his gifts of pearls as a symbol of his superiority and power. Her duty finally accomplished, Hannah returns to Salem but not before paying her deepest tributes to Bhagmati, her Indian Hester Manning. However, this rechristening of Bhagmati is viewed as "the ultimate colonization"[25] by Hema Nair.

Hannah's journey to India is fraught with images of adventure, action and passion. She returns to her native land, not as a reformed American but a rebel living on the fringes of society. Like Jasmine, Hannah finds final contentment and joy in the adapted land and it is the morality of this land that Hannah carries along with her. Bharati Mukherjee describes *The Holder of the World*, as a "post-modern historical novel"[26] but at its most basic level, it is a novel of expatriation, of a quest not only to geographically diverse lands but to culturally variant societies as well. Hannah's life succeeds in questioning and discovering new ways of defining reality in a world which was essentially orthodox. Hema Nair is assertive in her comment :

> Hannah is a stunning creation, a bold mind striving for identity in strange surroundings, a timeless creature trying to survive in a rigid, inexorably defined society.[27]

The novel ends with Hannah's return journey to Salem where she locates her mother from a mental asylum and brings up her "black" daughter Pearl Singh and fearlessly stays in Salem all her life — alongwith her mother's five half Nipmuc children; and Beigh Master's tracking the most perfect diamond in the world the Emperor's Tear.

Thus, *The Holder of the World* portrays an entirely different picture of jostling of cultures — the Eastern and the Western and the result thereof. Hannah Easton's voyage is mental and 'interior' rather than physical. It seems that the movement of the narrative is circular since the story ends in the same vein as it opens but the person (Hannah) does not remain the same. Her whole personality goes under a sea-change during her restless moves from Salem to Stepney, Coromandel to Devgad and then back to Salem :

> In one rainy season, Hannah Legge had gone from woollen clad English married woman on the Coromandel Coast to pregnant sari-wearing bibi of a raja; a murderer (she murders Morad Farah, one of the Great Generals of Aurangzeb), a widow, a peacemaker turned prisoner of the most powerful man in India .... She wasn't Hannah anymore; she was Mukta, Bhagmati's word for 'pearl' (p. 271).

Hannah Easton burries her Puritan past and emerges as a real fighter for life. The love she has got from Raja Jadav Singh makes her reckless and daring. Now she can face the holder of the world, the 'Alamgir', the Great Mughal Emperor Aurangzeb, with courage and confidence. Her plea before the Emperor to stop the war against her lover is a superb piece of oratory :

> I have come late in my life to the feeling of love. Love for a man, love for a place, love for a people. They are not Devgad people or Roopconda people, not Hindu people or Muslim people, not Sunni or Shia, priests or untouchables, servants or kings. If all is equal in the eye of Brahma as the Hindus say, if Allah is all-seeing and all-merciful as you say, then who has committed atrocities on the children, the women, the old people? Who has poisoned the hearts of men? (p. 268).

Ultimately she wins the heart of "Alamgir" who hails her with a very precious title : "For your white skin, for the luster of your spirit, for the one-in-a-lakh, I give you these pearls. I call you Precious-as-Pearl" (p. 270).

Beign Masters, the narrator, passes the final judgement about Hannah's character and personality when she acknowledges :

> Wherever she stayed... she would have changed history for she was one of those extraordinary lives through which history runs a four-lane highway (p. 189).

Mukherjee's latest novel *Leave It to Me* appeared in 1997. This work continues the theme of immigration and in a way, it completes the trilogy beginning with *Jasmine*. Reviewing it in *The Hindu* Shalini Gupta writes :

> In her latest novel, "Leave It to Me," about hitting the hippie-trail in post-hippie America, Mukherjee views life from the outside. Behind plastic, unauthenticated facades, the reality crumbles into a Karma-Cola as tacky as "cosmic glue."[28]

The protagonist is a Eurasian orphan, Debbie Devi who is adopted by an upstate New York family of Italian origin. Born in India and raised as an adopted child, Devi Dee travels through America to find her bio-mom. By the time she has arrived in San Francisco and taken up with a band of aging ex-hippies and a psychotic Vietnam Vet, her identity crisis looms large. It leads her to track down her bio-parents in Laxmipur, Devigaon, India, and the orphanage where she was raised — the Gray Sisters — "Soeurs Grises" — Sore Grease — in Mount Abu. She learns from Fred, her hired detective, that her mother was the hippie follower of a sex-age guru, and her father the founder of the ashram, serial killer Romeo Hawk/Haque. The offspring of this unlikely liaison, Devi Dee — presumed missing or dead — is saved by nuns and shipped abroad to America, where she is raised as the adopted child of the DiMartino family. Twenty-three years later, having graduated from Suny, Albany, she sets out to seek her bio-mom in off-beat California.

> Who but a foundling has the moral right to seize not just a city, but a neighbourhood, and fashion a block or two

> of it into home? When you inherit nothing, you are entitled to everything.

The above statement quoted from the novel makes the predicament of the protagonist crystal-clear. Again here Mukherjee deals with the reality of 'Time-Travel.' An individual grappling with different culture around the globe to find his real identity. Shalini Gupta observes :

> A Kaleidoscopic wheel of a book, "Leave It to Me" reveals the scars of the beat generation, whose legacy to its survivors is as dangerous as shifting continental plates. Mukherjee shuttles between time and space zones to create a dichotomy "as wise as the San Andreas fault." The novel's sex and violence rip from the grandstands to centre-stage and the maelstrom engulfs all.[29]

The foregoing analysis of three novels *Jasmine*, *The Holder of the World* and *Leave It to Me* written by Bharati Mukherjee in the recent phase of her creative career beginning since 1989 shows that the theme of cross cultural confrontation continues to be her preoccupation. Her protagonists, notwithstanding their cultural and racial roots, invariably try to reach out to larger humanity and this lends a positive trait to their personality. One looks for something still more engaging in Bharati Mukherjee's next work of art.

REFERENCES

1. Bharati Mukherjee. *Jasmine* (New York : Grove Weidenfeld, 1989), p. 3.
2. Malashri Lal. "Bharati Mukherjee : The 'Maximalist Credo" in K.N. Awasthi, ed. *Contemporary Indian English Fiction : An Anthology of Essays* (New Delhi : ABS Publications, 1993), p. 59.
3. Samir Dayal. "Creating, Preserving, Destroying : Violence in Bharati Mukherjee's *Jasmine*," in Emmanuel S. Nelson, ed. *Bharati Mukherjee : Critical Perspectives* (New York : Garland Publishing, 1993), p. 71.
4. Jaiwanti Dimri. "From Marriage to Murder : A Comparative Study of Bharati Mukherjee's *Wife* and *Jasmine*," in Suman Bala, ed. *American Literature Today* (New Delhi : Prestige Books, 1994), p. 173.
5. Pushpa N. Parekh. "Telling her Tale : Narrative Voice and Gender Roles in Bharati Mukherjee's *Jasmine*," in Emmanuel S. Nelson, ed. *Bharati Mukherjee : Critical Perspectives*, *op. cit*, p. 113.
6. *Ibid.*, p. 113.

7. Alpina Sharma Knippling. "Toward an Investigation of the Subaltern in Bharati Mukherjee's *The Middleman and Other Stories* and *Jasmine*," in Emmanuel S. Nelson, ed. *Bharati Mukherjee : Critical Perspectives*, *op. cit*, p. 153.
8. Michael Connel, Grearson Jessi and Grimes Tom. "An Interview with Bharati Mukheriee," *Iowa Review* 20, 3(1990), 18.
9. Pushpa N. Parekh. *op.* cit., p. 117.
10. T. Padma. "From Acculturation to Self -Actualization : Diasporal Dream in Bharati Mukherjee's *Jasmine,*" in R.K. Dhawan and L.S.R. Krishna Sastry, eds. *Commonwealth Writing : A Study in Expatriate Experience* (New Delhi : Prestige, 1994), p. 84.
11. Samir Dayal. "Creating, Preserving, Destroying : Violence in Bharati Mukherjee's *Jasmine*," in Emmanuel S. Nelson, ed. *Bharati Mukherjee : Critical Perspectives*, *op. cit*, p. 77.
12. Michael Connell, *et al.* "An Interview with Bharati Mukherjee," p. 25.
13. *Ibid*, p. 19.
14. Indira Bhatt. "Bharati Mukherjee's *Jasmine* : An Immigrant's Attempt at Assimilations," in Suman Bala, ed. *American Literature Today*, *op. cit.*, p. 179.
15. *Ibid.*, p. 177.
16. Sarah Curtis. "All-American Indian," *Times Literary Supplement*, 27 April 1990, 436.
17. Malashri Lal. "Bharati Mukherjee : The 'Maximalist Credo'" in K.N. Awasthi, ed. *Contemporary Indian English Fiction : An Anthology of Essays*, *op. cit.*, p. 63.
18. Arshia Sattar. "A Review of *The Holder of the World*," *The Sunday Times*, 20 March 1994, p.6.
19. Quoted in Shakuntala Bharvani, "Bharati Mukherjee's *The Holder of the World*" in R.K. Dhawan, ed. *Indian Women Novelists*, Vol. III (Delhi : Prestige, 1995), p. 190.
20. Quoted on the cover page of the dust-jacket of *The Holder of the World* (New York : Alfred A. Knopf, 1993; Indian reprint, New Delhi : Viking, 1993).
21. Uma Parameswaran. "A Review of *The Holder of the World," World Literature Today*. 68, 3(1994), 637.
22. Arshia Sattar, *op. cit.*, p. 6.
23. Shakuntala Bharvani. "Bharati Mukherjee's *The Holder of the World*," *op. cit.*, p. 192.
24. Sandhya Rao Mehta. "The Utmost Coasts Abroad : Hannah Easton's Quest in *The Holder of the World*," in R.K. Dhawan, ed. *Indian Women Novelists*, Vol. 3, *op. cit.*, p. 197.

25. Hema Nair. "A Puritan in A Mughal Court," *The Toronto Review*, 12, 2 (Winter-Spring 1994), p. 106.
26. N.P. Krishna Kumar. "An Interview with Bharati Mukheriee," *Indian Express*, 13 Sept. 1992, p.6.
27. Hema Nair. "A Puritan in a Mughal Court," *op. cit.*, p. 106.
28. Shalini Gupta. "A Kaleidoscopic Wheel," *The Hindu* (Sunday), 19 Oct 1997, p. XX.
29. *Ibid.*

6

The Final Estimate

This exhaustive analysis of Bharati Mukherjee's fictional writings undertaken in the preceding chapters from a cultural perspective demonstrates that she has addressed herself to all the issues associated with expatriate experience. By choosing her protagonists from all parts of the world having divergent ethnic, religious and cultural preoccupations, she has attempted to explore the multiplicity of this theme which is centred in their struggles to outgrow inherited values. With her evolving creative vision the canvas of her thematic content enlarges and the complexity of cultural assimilation acquires a new dimension.

Mukherjee invariably focuses upon sensitive protagonists who lack a firm sense of cultural identity and, are natural victims of racism, sexism and numerous forms of social oppression. The beauty of much of her fiction lies in its being informed by her personal experiences. A peculiar sense of involvement bordering on total identification with the characters lends her novels a flavour rarely found among expatriate writers. She achieves a dispassionate objectivity through understatements and ironic observations. She feels for her suffering protagonists, at times empathises with them but seldom fails to underline their human vulnerability. Though she has herself undergone the traumatic process of acculturation, she has not allowed her prejudices to infect her art.

The very philosophy of an expatriate artist is one of concern, of apprehension and of looking at things critically. In her first novel, *The Tiger's Daughter*, Mukherjee draws a satirical portrait of Indian society from the perspective of her protagonist. Tara Banerjee, though a young expatriate, not fully accustomed to

American set up is remarkably estranged from the morals and values of her native land. She registers the frailties and contradictions of her ancestral way of life in a peculiar fashion and the close of the novel leaves ample scope for the reader to ponder over her predicament. Mukherjee's second novel, *Wife* is a psychological study of Dimple, a young woman from Calcutta, and of her problems in settling down in New York with her new husband. Brought up to be passive and dependent as per Indian standards of womanhood she lacks the inner resources to cope with the fear and challenging situations and ultimately descends into unexpected violence. It is to the credit of her creator that Dimple wins our attention and sympathy inspite of herself and her circumstances.

The second phase of Mukherjee's creative pilgrimage, conveniently called the one of Transition, saw the publication of her two major works — *Darkness* and *The Middleman and Other Stories*. While building-up her stories round the deep-rooted racism in Canada, she has ingeniously underscored the hostility between the nation's white majority and its various ethnic sub-cultures. One pertinently recalls here Eliot's idea of National Culture with a host of satellite cultures in a meaningful correspondence between the two. The stories collected in *Darkness* underline the pathos in the life of South-Asian, African and Caribbean immigrants. It is to the credit of Mukherjee that some of these tales are related from the perspective of white people as well, quite a few of whom betray their disapproval of prevalent norms. Within a small but intensive scope of a short story Mukherjee contrives plots to convey her message in a telling way. Her characters like Nafeesa, Angela and Jasmine leave deep imprints on the reader's psyche and goad him time and again to dilate on their situations in moments of silence. In view of her sharp observations and stylistic elegance as manifested in these stories, Mukherjee's following claim does not appear very tall :

> I see my "immigrant" stories replicated in a dozen American cities, and instead of seeing my Indianness as a fragile identity to be preserved against obliteration (or worse, a "visible" disfigurement to be hidden), I see it now as a set of fluid identities to be celebrated ("Introduction," *Darkness*, p. 3).

And she does celebrate 'fluid identities' which are her central creative impulse.

Of the three works written in her recent phase titled Immigration — *Jasmine*, *The Holder of the World* and *Leave It to Me* — *Jasmine* has been warmly received as a creative work of rare imaginative potential. Through her protagonist Jasmine, Mukherjee traces the significant milestones of an immigrant's final absorption in an adopted cultural milieu. In her indefatigable determination to carve her way from a mosaic of disheartening events, Jasmine exhibits manliness of no mean proportions :

> No one to call to, no one to disturb us. Just me and the man. Who had raped me, the man I had murdered. The room looked like a slaughterhouse. Blood had congealed on my hands, my chin, my breasts ... for the second time in three months, I was in a room with a slain man, my body bloodied. I was walking death. Death incarnate (p. 119).

A perceptive reader, however, does feel at times that the qualities attributed to Jasmine are exaggerated, may be out of Mukherjee's unqualified sympathies for her protagonist.

If Jasmine's story moves between Hasnapur, Florida, New York and California, the narrative of *The Holder of the World* is much larger in terms of time and space. Mukherjee imaginatively forges a link between the seventeenth century Mughal India and the contemporary Puritan American experience. While the content of earlier fictional writings has a fixed locale the story in *The Holder of the World* testifies to Mukherjee's artistic competence to fictionalise history. In her recent work *Leave It to Me*, Mukherjee reverts to her earlier obsession with an exile's agony. Its protagonist Debbie Dee, an Indian girl raised by an Italian upstate family in off beat California, comes to India in search of her roots. Interestingly enough Mukherjee's first protagonist Tara Banerjee leaves for States to ascertain her identity while her last protagonist, till date, Debbie Dee leaves America for India on a similar mission. Since both of them are of Indian origin, they supplement each other's odysseous exposure to unknown milieus.

Mukherjee started her creative work at a time when the Feminist movement was at its peak in the West and she was expected to articulate gender conflicts in an unequivocal way. Within the limited range of the present project, it can be observed that an ingrained Indianness weighs very highly on Mukherjee's psyche and she avoids grappling with this controversial issue. This impression is also corroborated by the behaviour of her women protagonists who are quite docile and submissive at least to one person in the tumults of their life experiences. They do wrestle with their problems, engage themselves in finding solutions for them but rarely try to dominate their male counterparts in purely feminist terms. Another possible explanation might be Mukherjee's over-riding creative urge to unravel an expatriate's dilemma to the total neglect of other concerns.

The majority of Mukherjee's fictional characters display an undying drive to build up life with fragments, howsoever fragile they might be, and thus they express their affirmation to life. In trying alternatives they do sometimes appear abnormal in their behaviour but this trait should be viewed from the angle of their innate bid to live life on their own terms. Writing in an atmosphere marked by sex and violence Mukherjee's works, seldom border on obscenity which again explains the constraints of her Indian roots despite avowed links with traditional American writers. The nuances of Indian cultural life provide a living ambience to Bharati Mukherjee, sometimes accepted, and at times, even revolted against but they are invariably her terms of reference to perceive and penetrate the Western ethos.

Select Bibliography

PRIMARY SOURCES

Novels

The Tiger's Daughter. Boston : Houghton Miffin, 1972.

Wife. Boston : Houghton Miffin, 1975.

Jasmine. New York : Grove Weidenfeld, 1989.

The Holder of the World. New York : Alfred A. Knopf, 1993.

Leave It to Me. London : Chatto and Windus, 1997.

Short Stories

Darkness. Toronto : Penguin, 1985.

The Middleman and Other Stories. New York : Grove Press, 1988.

Non-Fiction

Kautilya's Concept of Diplomacy : A New Interpretation. Calcutta : Minerva, 1976.

Literary Essays

"Response : American Fiction. *Salmagundi*, 50-51" (Fall 1980 Winter 1981), 151-71.

"An Invisible Woman." *Saturday Night*, 96 (March 1981), 36-40.

"Immigrant Writing : Give Us Your Maximalists." *The New York Times Book Review*, 28 August 1988, 28-29.

Works in Collaboration

(a) *With Clark Blaise* :

Days and Nights in Calcutta, New York : Doubleday, 197.

Screenplay — 1991.

The Sorrow and Terror : The Haunting Legacy of Air India Tragedy. Toronto : Viking, 1987.

(b) *With Robert Boyers* :

"A Conversation with V.S. Naipaul." *Salmagundi*, 54 (Fall 1981), 4-22.

SECONDARY SOURCES

Ashcroft, Bill *et al. The Empire Writes Back*, London : Routledge, 1989, p. 195.

Asnani, Shyam M. and Rajpal, Deepika. "Identity Crisis in *The Nowhere Man and Wife*." *Language Forum*, 1-2 (January-December 1992), 38-47.

Banerjee, Debjani. "In the Presence of History : The Representation of Past and Present Indias in Bharati Mukherjeels Fiction," in Nelson Emmanuel S., ed. *Bharati Mukherjee : Critical Perspectives*, New York and London : Garland Publishing, 1993, pp. 161-80.

Bharvani, Shakuntala. "Bharati Mukherjee's *The Holder of the World*," in Dhawan, R.K., ed. *Indian Women Novelists*, Vol. 3, New Delhi : Prestige, 1995, pp. 190-92.

Bhatt, Indira. "Bharati Mukherjee's *Jasmine* : An Immigrants Attempt at Assimilation," in Bala, Suman, ed. *American Literature Today*. New Delhi : Prestige, 1994, pp. 176-80

Bose, Brinda. "A Question of Identity : Where Gender, Race, and America meet in Bharati Mukherjee," in Nelson, Emmanuel S., ed. *Bharati Mukherjee : Critical Perspectives* pp. 47-63.

Boxill, Anthony. "Women and Migration in Some Short Stories of Bharati Mukherjee and Neil Bissoondath." The Literary Half-Yearly, 32.2 (July 1991), 43-50.

Carb, Alison B. "An Interview with Bharati Mukherjee." *The Massachusetts Review*, Winter 1988-1989, pp. 645-54.

Choudhury, Enakshi. "Images of Women in Bharati Mukherjee's Novels," in Anand, T.S., ed. *Literary Voice*, 2 (Oct. 1995), Ludhiana : Academic Association Trust, 81-87.

Chellappan, K. "The Concept of National Literature in India and Canada : A Comparison," in Ramamurti, K.S., ed. *Canadian Literature and Society*, New Delhi : Pencraft International, 1996, pp. 88-97.

Chua, C.L. "Passages from India : Migrating to America in the Fiction of V.S. Naipaul and Bharati Mukherjee," in Nelson, Emmanuel S., ed. *Reworlding : The Literature of the Indian Diaspora*, New York : Greenwood Press, 1992, pp. 51-61.

Coates, John. "Bharati Mukherjee," *Chicago Tribune*, 17 July 1989.

Connell, Michael, *et al.* "An Interview with Bharati Mukherjee," *Iowa Review*, 20.3 (1990), 7-32.

Crane, Ralph J. "Bharati Mukherjee" in Henderson, Lesley, ed. *Contemporary Novelists*, Chicago and London : St. James Press, 1991, pp. 670-71.

Curtis, Sarah. "All American Indian." *Times Literary Supplement*, 27 April 1990, 436.

Davidar, David. "The Immigrant Native." The Indian Express, 19 February 1989, p. 5.

Dayal, Samir. "Creating, Preserving, Destroying : Violence in Bharati Mukherjee's *Jasmine*" in Nelson, Emmanuel S., ed. *Bharati Mukherjee : Critical Perspectives*. pp. 65-88.

Desai, Anita. "Outcasts," *London Magazine* 25, 9 and 10 (December 1985 and January 1986), 143-46.

Dimri, Jaiwanti. "From Marriage to Murder : A Comparative Study of Bharati Mukherjee's *Wife* and *Jasmine,*" in Bala, Suman, ed. *American Literature Today*, pp. 170-75.

Eliot, T.S. *Notes Towards the Definition of Culture*, London : Faber, 1948.

Eagleton, Terry. "Eliot and a Common Culture," in Martin, Graham, ed. *Eliot in Perspective* (London : Macmillan, 1970), p. 286.

Gomez, Christine. "The On-Going Quest of Bharati Mukherjee from Expatriation to Immigration," in Dhawan, R.K. ed. *Indian Women Novelists*, Vol. 3, New Delhi : Prestige, 1995, pp. 71-87.

——. "From Expatriation to Immigration : The Quest of Bharati Mukherjee with Special Reference to *Darkness*," in Ramamurti, K.S., ed. *Canadian Literature and Society*, New Delhi : Pencraft International, 1996, pp. 131-40.

Gorra, Michael. "Call It Exile Call It Immigration," *New York Times Book Review*, 10 September 1989, p. 9.

Grewal, Gurleen. "Born Again American : The Immigrant Consciousness in *Jasmine,*" in Nelson, Emmanuel S., ed. *Bharati Mukherjee : Critical Perspectives*, pp. 181-96.

Gupta, Shalini. "A Kaleidoscopic Wheel," *The Hindu* (Sunday), 19 October 1997, p. 20.

Hancock, Geoff. "An Interview with Bharati Mukherjee," *Canadian Fiction Magazine*, 59(1987), 30-44.

Inamdar, F.A. "Man-Woman Relationship *in The Tiger's Daughter* and *Wife*," in Awasthi, K.N., ed. *Contemporary Indian English Fiction*, New Delhi : ABS Publication, 1993, pp. 65-73.

Indira, S. "Splintered Self : An Approach to Bharati Mukherjee's Wife," in Dhawan, R.K. *et al.*, eds. *Commonwealth Writing*, New Delhi : Prestige, 1994, p. 72-76.

——. "*Jasmine* : An Odyssey of Unhousement and Enhousement," in Dhawan, R.K. *et al.*, eds. *Commonwealth Writing*, pp. 86-90.

Jain, Jasbir. "Foreignness of Spirit : The World of Bharati Mukherjee's Novels," *Journal of Indian Writing in English*, 13, 2 (July 1985), 12-19.

Jameson, Fredric. *Post-Modernism or The Cultural Logic of Late Capitalism*, London and New York : Verso, 1991, p. 6.

Joshi, Arun. *The Foreigner*, New Delhi : Hind Pocket Books, 1968.

Kaye, Melanic. "Review of *Jasmine*," *Women's Review of Books* (April 1990), 7.

Khan, M.Q. "The New Technique of the Non-Fiction Novel in Travel Writings of V.S. Naipaul and Bharati Mukherjee," in Singh, A.K., ed. *Contemporary Indian Fiction in English*, New Delhi : Creative, 1993, pp. 70-83.

Kirpal, Viney. *The Third World Novel of Expatriation : A Study of Emigre Fiction by Indian, West African* and *Caribbean Writers*, New Delhi : Sterling, 1989, p. 165.

Klass, Rosanne. "Indian Wife Lives Soap-Opera Life." *MS*, October (1975), 83-84 & 88.

Knippling, Alpana Sharma. "Toward an Investigation of the Subaltern in Bharati Mukherjee's *The Middleman and Other Stories* and *Jasmine,*" in Nelson, Emmanuel S., ed., *Bharati Mukherjee : Critical Perspectives*, pp. 143-159.

Koening, Rhoda. "Passage From India," *New York Times*, 25 September 1989, p. 132.

Krishnakutty, Gita. "A Review of Bharati Mukherjee's *Wife*," *Literary Criterion*, 26, 1 (1991), 88-89.

Kumar, N.P. Krishna. "India is in Touch with Us," *The Indian Express* (Sunday Magazine), 13 Sept. 1992, p. 6.

Kumar, Nagendra. "Cross-Cultural Conflict in Bharati Mukherjee's *Jasmine*" *Rajashtan University Studies in English*, 24 (1993-96), 47-53.

Lal, Malashri. "Bharati Mukherjee : The Maximalist Credo" in Awasthi, K.N., ed. *Contemporary Indian English Fiction : An Anthology of Essays*, New Delhi : ABS. Publications, 1993, pp. 55-64.

Leong, Liew-Geok. "Bharati Mukherjee," in Ross, Robert L., ed., *International Literature in English : Essays on the Modern Writers*, New York : St. James Press, 1991, pp. 487-500.

Levin, Martin. "A Review of Bharati Mukherjee's *Wife*," *New York Times Book Review*, 8 June 1975, pp. 17 and 20.

Mandel, Ann. "Bharati Mukherjee," in New, W.H., ed. *Dictionary of Literary Biography : Canadian Writers Since 1960* Vol. 60, Detroit : Gale Research Company, 1986, pp. 266-69.

Mazumdar, S. "The Hollow Men and Women," *Financial Express*, 6 May (1990), 10.

Mehta, Shandhya Rao. "The Utmost Coasts Abroad : Hannah Easton's Quest in *The Holder of the World,*" in Dhawan, R.K., ed. *Indian Women Novelists*, pp. 193-98.

Melwani, Lavina. "The Best of Two Worlds," Asia Magazine, 8-10 December (1989), 34-36.

Moline, Karen. "Passage from India : Award Winning Novelist Bharati Mukherjee," *Harper's Bazar* (Australia), Autumn 1990, p. 219.

Nabar, Vrinda. "The Way I Write has Changed Dramatically," *The Sunday Times*, 31 December, 1995.

Nair, Hema. "A Puritan in a Mughal Court." *The Toronto Review*, 12, 2 (Winter-Spring 1994), 104-07.

Nazareth, Peter. "Total Vision," *Canadian Literature* (Fall 1986), 184-91.

Nelson, Cecil L. "New Englishes, New Discourses : New Speech acts," *World Englishes*, 10, 3 (1991), 317-23.

Nelson, Emmanuel S. *Bharati Mukherjee : Critical Perspectives*, New York and London : Garland Publishing, 1993.

Nikam, N.A. *Some Aspects of Indian Culture*. Shimla : Indian Institute of Advanced Studies, 1973, pp. 1-2.

Nityanandam, Indira. "Yasmine Gooneratne's *A Change of Skies* and Bharati Mukherjee's *Jasmine* : The Immigrant Experience in Australia and the USA," in Dhawan, R.K. *et al.*, eds. *Commonwealth Writing*, pp. 50-54.

Oh Calcutta! Bharati Mukherjee's *The Tiger's Daughter, Times Literary Supplement*, 29 June 1973, p. 736.

Padma, T. "From Acculturation to Self -Actualization : Diasporal Dream in Bharati Mukherjee's *Jasmine,*" in Dhawan, R.K. *et al.*, eds. *Commonwealth Writing*, pp. 77-85.

Pandya, Sudha. "Bharati Mukherjee's *Darkness* : Exploring the Hyphenated Identity," *Quill*, December (1990), 68-73.

Parameswaran, Uma. "What Price Expatriation?" in Niven, Alastair ed. *The Commonwealth Writer Overseas : Themes of Exile and Expatriation*. Brussels : Libraire Marcel Didier, 1976, p. 41.

——. "A Review of Bharati Mukherjee's *Darkness*," *World Literature Today*, Summer (1986), 520-21.

——. "Bharati Mukherjee's *The Middleman and Other Stories* : A Review," *World Literature Today*, 64, 4 (1990), 363.

——. "Bharati Mukherjee's *Jasmine* — A Review," *World Literature Today*, 64, 4 (1990), 698-99.

——. "A Review of Bharati Mukherjee's *The Holder of the World*," *World Literature Today*, 68, 3 (1994), 636-37.

Patekh, Pushpa N. "Telling Her Tale : Narrative Voice and Gender

Roles in Bharati Mukherjee's *Jasmine,*" in Nelson, Emmanuel S., ed. *Bharati Mukherjee : Critical Perspectives* pp. 109-26.

Pati, Mitali R. "Love and the Indian Immigrant in Bharati Mukherjee's Short Fiction," in Nelson, Emmanuel S., ed. *Bharati Mukherjee : Critical Perspectives*, pp.197-211.

Pinto, Jerry. "Bharati But American," *The Sunday Times*, 5 January 1997, p. II

Powers, Janet M. "Sociopolitical Critique as Indices And Narrative Codes in Bharati Mukherjee's *Wife* and *Jasmine,*" in Nelson, Emmanuel S., ed., *Bharati Mukherjee : Critical Perspectives*, pp. 89-08.

Raban, Jonathan. "Savage Boulevards, Easy Streets," *The New York Times*, 19 June (1988), 21.

Rai, Sudha. *V. S. Naipaul : A Study in Expatriate Sensibility*, New Delhi : Heinemann, 1982, pp. 15-16.

Rajeshwar, M. "Sado-Masochism as a Literary Device in Bharati Mukherjee's *Wife*" in Dhawan, R.K. *et al*., eds. *Commonwealth Writing*, pp. 61-71.

Ramchandra, Ragini. "Bharati Mukherjee's *Wife* : An Assessment," *The Literary Criterion*, 26 (March 1991), 56-67.

Rao, A.V. Krishna. "From Expatriation to Immigration : The Case of Bharati Mukherjee," in Dhawan, R.K., ed. *Indian Women Novelists*, pp. 88-102.

Rao, K.S. Narayan. "Bharati Mukherjee's *Wife* — A Review," *Books Abroad*, Spring (1976), 474-75.

Roy, Anindyo. "The Aesthetics of an (Un)Willing Immigrant : Bharati Mukherjee's *Days and Nights in Calcutta,*" in Nelson, Emmanuel S., ed. *Bharati Mukerjee : Critical Perspectives*, pp. 127-41.

Rushdie, Salman. *Shame*, New York : Aventura, 1983, p. 24.

——. *Imaginary Homelands : Essays and Criticism*, London : Granata Books, 1991, p. 19.

Rustomji-Kerns, Roshni. "Expatriates, Immigrants and Literature : Three South-Asian Women Writers," *The Massachusetts Review*, 29.4 (Winter 1988-1989), 655-65.

——. "Mukherjee, Bharati," *The Oxford Companion to English Literature* (1995), 588-89.

St. Andrews, B.A. "Co-Wanderers Kogawa and Mukherjee : New Immigrant Writers," *World Literature Today*, 66, 1 (1992), 56-58.

Sanborn, Kristin Carter. "We Murder Who We Were : *Jasmine* and the Violence of Identity," *American Literature*, 66.3 (1994), 573-93.

Sandler, Linda. "Violence as a Device of Problem-Solving," *Saturday Night*, 90, 5 (October 1975), 75-76.

Sathiah, K. "A Review of Bharati Mukherjee's *Wife*," *Literary Criterion*, 26, 1 (1991), 89-90.

Sathupati, Prasanna Shree. "Psychotic Violence of Dimple in Bharati Mukherjee's *Wife*," in Dhawan, R.K., ed. *Indian Women Novelists*, pp. 110-16.

Sattar, Arshia. "Review of Bharati Mukherjee's *The Holder of the World*," *The Sunday Times* (Sunday Review), 20 March 1994, p. 6.

Sengupta, C. "Asian Protagonists in Bharati Mukherjee's *The Middleman and Other Stories*," *Language Forum*, 1-2 (Jan-Dec 1992), 148-56.

——. "The Broken Pitcher and the Third Eye : Indian Sensibility in Bharati Mukherjee's *Jasmine*," in Pathak, R.S., ed. *Indianization of English Language and Literature*, New Delhi : Bahri Publication, 1994, pp. 181-91.

Sengupta, C. "Feminine Mystique in Bharati Mukherjee's *Jasmine*," in Dass, Veena Noble, *et al.*, eds. *Fiction of the Nineties*, New Delhi : Prestige, 1994, pp. 197-204.

Sharma, Maya Manju. "The Inner World of Bharati Mukherjee : From Expatriate to Immigrant," in Nelson, Emmanuel S. ed. *Bharati Mukherjee : Critical Perspectives*, pp. 3-22.

Shinde, Shobha. "Cross-Cultural Crisis in Bharati Mukherjee's *Jasmine* and *The Tiger's Daughter*," in Dhawan, R.K. *et al.*, eds. *Commonwealth Writing*, pp. 55-60.

Shirwadkar, Meena. *Image of Women in the Indo-Anglian Novel*, New Delhi : Sterling, 1979.

Shulman, Polly. "Home Truths," *Times Literary Supplement,* 66 (June 1988), 19.

Sicherman, Carol. "Transport Me... into the Hearts of Men : Bharati Mukherjee's *Darkness*," *Kunapipi*, 14, 3 (1992), 83-98.

Sivaramkrishna, M. "Bharati Mukherjee" in Prasad, M.S., ed. *Indian English Novelists*, New Delhi : Sterling, 1982 pp. 71-86.

Sivaraman, S. "*Jasmine* : A Search for Alternate Realities," in Pathak, R.S. , ed. *Recent Indian Fiction*. New Delhi : Prestige, 1994, pp. 210-18.

Steinberg, Sybil. "Bharati Mukherjee : PW Interviews," *Publishers Weekly*, 25 August 1989, pp. 46-47.

Steiner, George. *Extra Territorial : Papers on Language and Literature*, London : Faber, 1968, pp. 10-11.

Stone, Carole. "The Short Fictions of Bernard Malamud and Bharati Mukherjee," in Nelson, Emmanuel S., ed. *Bharati Mukherjee : Critical Perspectives*, pp. 213-26.

Sujatha, S. "The Theme of Disintegration : A Comparative Study of Anita Desai's *Cry, the Peacock* and Bharati Mukherjee's *Wife,*" in Dhawan, R.K. *et al.* eds. *Commonwealth Writing : A Study in Expatriate Experience*, pp. 45-49.

Tikoo, S.K. "The American Dream : Immigration and Transformation Theme in *The Middleman and Other Stories,*" in Dhawan, R.K., ed. *Indian Women Novelists*, New Delhi : Prestige, 1992, p. 219.

Tompkins, Jane P. *Reader-Response Criticism*, Baltimore : John Hopkins University, 1980.

Uma, Alladi. *Woman and Her Family : Indian and Afro-American — A Literary Perspective*, New Delhi : Sterling, 1989.

Venkateshwaran, Pramila. "Bharati Mukherjee as Autobiographer," in Nelson, Emmanuel S., ed. *Bharati Mukherjee : Critical Perspectives*, pp. 23-45.

Wade-Sant, Arvindra, *et al.* "Refashioning the Self : Immigrant Women in Bharati Mukherjee's New World," *Studies in Short Fiction*, 29.1 (Winter 1992), 11-17.